On… a Planetary Court of Justice

On… a Planetary Court of Justice

William W Morgan

BookSurge Publishing LLC,
an Amazon.com Company
Universal Salvage
Specialists in Dying Civilizations
http://universal-salvage.org.uk

Other Books by the author:

Cowardly New World
<http://universal-salvage.org.uk/book_list.php>

An "Einstein" Thought Experiment
<http://universal-salvage.org.uk/book_list.php#ein>

The Biblical Flood
<http://universal-salvage.org.uk/book_list.php#flood>

On… Job Security: End of Unemployment & Poverty
<http://universal-salvage.org.uk/book_list.php#js>

On… Terrorism: Simple Cause & Cure
<http://universal-salvage.org.uk/book_list.php#on>

On… Democracy & Freedom: Mutually Exclusive Concepts
<http://universal-salvage.org.uk/book_list.php#demo>

Published by
BookSurge Publishing LLC,
an Amazon.com Company
Universal Salvage
Specialists in Dying Civilizations
239 S. Juniper Street
Escondido, CA 92025
U. S. A.
SAN: 850-4016

ISBN-13: 978-0-9778492-6-0 (paperbound)
Library of Congress Control Number: 2007901202
First Edition: February, 2007

Printed in the United States of America

Contents

Appendices

Cover

As with all the "On… [subject]" series of pamphlets at the moment, the front cover is essentially blank. No graphic. But it may not always be that way, so I will leave space for comments.

Gratitude

First and primarily gratitude must be given to my great and wonderful teacher Andrew J. Galambos (1924-1997). Who, among other things, taught me how to think. To understand the concept of positive history and "how to know you are right". To evaluate knowledge for rightness.

Galambos also introduced me to many other teachers. Those in the flow stream of history who have created new and useful knowledge and possibly tangible products. Those from Archimedes to Zemansky.[1] From the time of about 500 bce to yesterday and even today.

Next, and also at the top of the list, my great and wonderful wife. Who has intelligence, understanding and patience beyond measure. Putting up with an angry, cantankerous old man. She is a person of unique, indispensable qualities. My best friend in life.

There is another person to whom I owe a great amount of gratitude. His name is J. Stuart Snelson. He was the lecturer for my V-50 course. The first of Galambos' courses I attended.

Snelson had a great understanding of history. Of the history of science. And how science effects our thinking world. The importance of history and the concepts of rightness and importance in history. Of the importance of individual freedom to society and the quality of life for individuals.

Besides "the facts", he was also a very good speaker. Often explaining the same thing in several different ways to make sure you understood the significance of a concept to actual life. Presenting the first contact with Galambos' ideas, this could be of critical importance. Critical to a correct understanding of concepts that are important to our very survival as a specie.

Snelson was "open" and friendly. People found it easy to interact with him. This was often not the case with Galam-

---

1 Mark W Zemansky, one of the great thermodynamic scientists.

bos. Although please note that I am saying this with profound gratitude and affection to and for Galambos. And in the same sense I think of Newton.

Newton needed a spokesman. He was not "open" and friendly. It has been stated by people who knew Newton that he was not known to have smiled in their presence in five years. But the important thing is that the knowledge first be *created* and *then* disseminated. It is not important that the creator be "nice and friendly" unless by not being so their knowledge is lost. Or there is significant delay in getting it into the market.

The fact that Newton had no such spokesman is a major reason for his squabbles with Hooke and Leibniz. And probably accounts for the approximate 75 year delay in getting Newton's ideas into the market. Beginning to have a tangible effect on the lives of other thinking beings.

Editing this I notice I referred to Snelson as a "lecturer". This he was. But on reflection I realize he was also a *teacher.* Which is a much higher appellation. In fact, I believe that it and medical doctor are second in importance only to "innovator". Someone who creates new and useful products.

The innovator creates new and useful knowledge. But then it must be disseminated in such a way that others understand it. Else it is lost.

Which could have been the case with Galambos, who left almost nothing in writing. Leaving only the tape recordings of his lectures and a few short pamphlets. And if a person does not listen to the tapes with the understanding that there is something very extraordinary there, they may well understand nothing. Sadly, it was very easy to go to sleep listening to Galambos. And to get lost in his digressions.

In a sense Snelson "published" the ideas of Galambos, just as Edmund Halley published the ideas of Newton. The former verbally, the latter on paper.

Snelson may thus be seen as being crucial to the survival of the knowledge created by Galambos. And to the future understanding that Galambos' work was of signal importance to Homo sapiens.

If we survive as a specie it will be because Galambos' knowledge was not lost. And was implemented. And if so, a big reason for that will be because of Snelson's delivery of the knowledge. And I think we might then be able to say that Snelson would rank only slightly below Galambos in importance...?

Preface

There is much talk these days about trying politicians for their crimes. And some are being tried. There is talk about the proper courts and venues for such trials. Whether the criminals should be tried in their own political entity or in some supposedly "neutral" political entity.

There is often talk about "justice". But usually without defining it. If there is a definition it is quite long, not absolute and not very clear and useful.[2] There is talk of the possible penalties for the criminal. Usually this is either imprisonment for "life" or to be executed.

There is rarely thought of doing something that will prevent recurrence of the crime. Feeling that these things—the offenses—will inevitably happen. Perhaps because it is in the nature of the specie Homo sapiens. Which is not true.

It is not in the nature of "man", the specie. But in the defective societal system we have adopted for ourselves. Which allows for—even requires—retribution. Creating a closed-loop of violence and retribution. But we can get rid of this system and adopt one that works. That is easy.

As with all problems, it only requires the validation for *rightness* of the knowledge we are using. And, when that fails, the creation of new and useful knowledge to replace the failed hypotheses. And the implementation of this new and useful knowledge.

It also require *intellectual honesty.* Meaning that when cherished fallacies are shown to be incorrect, that they are no longer accepted and used.

---

2 With *absolute* meaning it is the only concept of rightness. That it is based on true premises and valid and logical thought processes. That the definition is therefore *right* on an absolute basis.

Chapter 1

A Planetary Court of Justice

Synopsis

Today there is a general outcry for an "International Court of Human Rights". Presumably based on enforcing the "Declaration of Human Rights" or whatever it is called.

But since no one on this planet seems to have and use a proper understanding of *justice, freedom, rightness* and the other operative words related to criminal activities they have little chance of creating a proper justice system.

This chapter provides the proper concept of such a system.

Background

I do not apologize for not knowing the correct name of various political documents purporting to describe and create a system of "human rights". Why?

Because such a document will be an outgrowth of politics and based on coercion. It will not have consistent definitions on which to base its case. Valid, absolute definitions of the main operative concepts and words. Such as justice, human rights, freedom and related concepts.

Further, it will depend on politicians and bureaucrats to make decisions. Rather than a concept of what is *right* on an absolute basis. The name is as irrelevant as the concept used.

An international court of justice would presumably protect people from injustice and offer recourse when and where there was injustice. Recourse from violations of their "human rights". But before this can be done it is necessary to define the operative terms involved with the process. Such as:

- Justice.
- Freedom.
- Human rights.

"But wait," you say. "This has already been done". Yes, I know that. Representatives for every political entity in the world—plus most individuals—have a definition for these words and the associated concept. There are about as many definitions as there are people. Some will be identical, others nearly the same. But this is not good enough. If the "court" is to serve all the people of the planet the definitions must be acceptable to all. They must be consistent and absolute.

Further, there is a problem with the word "international". Which should really be used with a hyphen, making it "inter-national". To make it clear that it is referring to activities between political entities. "Nations", or large, multi-tribal groupings. A primitive, failed concept.

We see the significance of this in Afghanistan and Iraq, which are artificial groupings of tribes. One of the major reasons that the concept of "nation" is not a valid concept. Another of course being that it offers no improvement over the concept of "tribe". Still having a tribal chief and witch doctor to control the lives and property of tribal members. A situation that has existed for millions of years. One that these millions of years of history shows us does not work. As it seeks to contravene the laws of nature. A subject that will be discussed later in the book.

But there is still the matter of definitions and semantic precision.

There is a reason why our specie has never solved even one of its societal problems. And why "technology" races ahead with new solutions by the minute. This is because of absolute definitions and semantic precision. This allows anyone, anywhere to propose valid solutions to technological problems. Because everyone uses the same definitions. Further, these definitions are consistent with the laws of nature. Upon which they are actually based. And have been shown by history to work. That if used, individuals can continuously create new and useful ideas and associated products and services.

The reason we have never solved any of our societal problems is because no one understands what anyone is saying. An individual says something, and each listener interprets it based on their own peculiar definition of the operative words. Everyone shakes their head in agreement or disagreement but no one has understood anything that was said. It is so bad that most people do not even listen. Their thoughts race ahead with their own definitions and have no idea of what the speaker was trying to say.

You can verify this by putting ten people in a room and asking them for a definition of some of the operative words used in what is commonly and incorrectly referred to as "social science" or "political science".

Neither of these is "science" in the sense of organized knowledge. And the result of "social science" is not "social" in the sense of improving the lives of individuals. And of course "political science" is an oxymoron. Politics and science—organized knowledge—are mutually exclusive concepts.

Confirming this, you will surely get ten definitions. Then as these are discussed, five or ten different definitions will emerge. You can not understand current problems and create new and useful knowledge to solve them with a situation such as this.

Please, this concept of definitions and semantic precision is very important. In its application to the knowledge related to the interaction of thinking beings. Important to our very survival as a specie. This is corroborated by the continuing, even increasing disorder in society. The fact that we are not solving any of out societal problems, and they are only getting worse.

Please, you must think about this…?

What is it that thinking beings want in life? I suggest it is the following:

- To be in total control of their own lives.

- To be able to fulfill their hopes and dreams for their life.
- To not have anyone interfere in their lives.
- To have justice.

To have recourse if there is interference in their life.

It is this last item that I envision as the reason for this discussion on a Planetary Court of Justice (PCOJ).

That if someone should interfere in your life—in the realization of your individual hopes and dreams for your life—that there will be some recourse. Perhaps mainly that the criminal will be known and there will be a chance for restitution. And that the system will tend to discourage people from interfering in the lives of others. That the deviant behavior will be known and attributed to the criminal. That they will gain nothing from this interference. And in fact will lose. They will lose time and money. Personal assets and resources. And that crime truly does not pay. But costs dearly.

And that any system that creates this condition is one that should be considered for use.

The justices of the court

There are no human "justices" in the sense of one or a few judges. Or of a formal court. They are not needed. All that is needed is a proper *concept* of justice. Of what is moral. For this it is necessary to define "justice" and "morality". And what is "moral". And the credit system and associated clearing houses. Those things that ensure a "seamless", true solution to the problem. A cure.[3]

To do this and understand the definitions we must start at the beginning. With the basics. What is basic when we speak of *justice* or *morality*? It is *property*. With credit to Galambos, property is basic to volitional life.[4] As the desire for its acqui-

---

3 With credit to Galambos, the definition of *cure* is: "The total and permanent cessation of all adverse symptoms".

4 Andrew J. Galambos (1924-1997). Creator of the Science of Volition and integrator of the Volitional Sciences.

sition and maximization is basic to and evidence of thinking life.

If individuals did not seek to acquire property they could not survive. They would not be "volitional". Not thinking beings. Not biased, discriminatory and prejudicial. I know: these all have bad images. Because people do not think.

To be *biased* merely means to have examined possibilities and have a preference. To *discriminate* is merely to think and make a choice. Whether it is a good one or not is another matter. To be *prejudiced* or prejudicial merely means you have already made up your mind on a subject. When this is based on valid and logical thought process, and the resulting action will be moral, then this is one of the higher examples of the activities for a thinking specie.

To discriminate. To be biased and prejudiced. It is only when you are intellectually dishonest that these are bad. Such as when you are a politician and use the police powers of the political state to enforce an intellectually dishonest action.

Without the desire to acquire property, the resulting society would not be a viable volitional (thinking) society. Even supposedly non-volitional animals seek property and its control. Such as in the territory of a bear or a wolf. They and many other animals will mark what they consider to be their territory. And woe be to the individual who seeks to invade their territory, "... for they shall receive justice". To learn more about this read *The Territorial Imperative* by Robert Ardrey.[5]

Definitions first start as a more or less arbitrary thing. An attempt to define something and see if it works. See if it makes sense, and allows a person to acquire more information and knowledge based on the definition. If not, it is changed. Fine-tuned until it does work. And others find its use helpful to them in creating new and useful knowledge. And evaluating existing knowledge.

---

5 Robert Ardrey, *The Territorial Imperative: A Personal Inquiry into the Animal Origins of Property and Nations* (Kodansha International, 1997).

Also, definitions—and semantic precision—are necessary for effective communication. Without them it is one person saying something based on *their* definition, and the other person "translating" the information based on *their* definition. Which is the way it was in what is commonly called "science", or better referred to as "technology", until the time of Isaac Newton.

The most important thing Newton did was to elaborate and elucidate a system for creating, evaluating, and accepting new information. And thus for creating new and useful knowledge. This was far more significant than his laws of optics or motion. To be able to know if you are right is necessary for the survival of a thinking specie.

This and his elegant if implicit statement that "the universe is comprehensible". That it is possible to create new and useful knowledge. As opposed to merely re-circulating and reinterpreting existing knowledge.

As was done in the Middle Ages—the Dark Ages—with the knowledge of Aristotle. Who would actually have been appalled at this. And as we do now with "social science" and religion.

The laws of motion and optics are necessary to create new and useful technology, but not for the survival of the specie.

With this concept people could interpret the laws of nature using commonly accepted definitions that approached—if not reached—the "absolute". Definitions that are valid regardless of time and place.

This system is what might be called "The Court of Right & Wrong". Or to be more positive, we need only say "The Court of Rightness". But in order to do this for our societal knowledge we must create or employ some definitions that will approach the absolute for *evaluating knowledge in the social sphere.* Which would be knowledge of what is right in the social sphere. In that area of knowledge related to the interaction of thinking beings.

We currently refer to this incorrectly as "social science".

It is not "social" in the result. Since it almost always degrades the quality of life for the individual. And is not "science" in the sense of organized knowledge.

For us to have effective communications you should temporarily accept these definitions. Simply for the purpose of understanding what I am saying. If in so doing you find them useful and believe they may be "right," then you might want to continue using them. If you do not find them useful then you should discard them.

I would encourage you to observe the world around you. See if the definitions presented are corroborated by history, current events and actions. To think about them before discarding them.

If we assume that "property" is basic to individual volitional life then we need a definition of this word and for its concept.

With credit to Galambos, who created the concept and definition, *property* is defined as:

"Individual life, and all non-procreative results thereof."[6]

It should be noted that explicit in this definition is the fact that an individual does not *own* their children. They are not property in that sense. A parent has a moral—and rational—obligation to guide a child to the point in life at which they can independently, morally, and rationally fulfill the obligations of individual thinking life. That they can differentiate between that action which is moral and rational or not so. Using the absolute, proper definition of that concept.

I will not go further into the epistemological basis for the preceding definition, nor a detailed elaboration of it, as this is done in other essays.

Further, Galambos described three types of property:

- Primordial.
- Primary.
- Secondary.

---

[6] Andrew J. Galambos (1924-1997). Creator of the Science of Volition and integrator of the Volitional Sciences.

The definitions of these terms are in Appendix A. I will also discuss them in the following chapter.

Chapter 2

Court Concepts

We must define certain concepts related to the establishment of a proper court. These will be much different than the usual political concepts. Since they are moral and rational concepts.

Primordial property

Primordial property might be thought of as the "life support system for the brain". The human brain being the thing that distinguishes Homo sapiens from all other animals on the planet. Providing us with the ability to engage in abstract thought. To think and reason. A person's own body. If they do not own it, who does? If someone other than you has control over *any* of your property—including the primordial property—this is the condition known as *slavery*. It is the operative definition of slavery. Think of the societal implications if a person does not own and is not in total control of their own body?

Galambos' definition of "primordial property" is:

"Individual life itself".

Primary property

The creation of "primary property" is a basic, distinguishing characteristic of a thinking being. In its most elegant form it is:

- Thinking of what is.
- Thinking of what might, can and should be.

In our very imperfect world I must add "... with the resulting action being moral and rational". Otherwise it is not elegant. Not adding to the qualify of life for the individual. Nor useful to the survival of the specie.

The definition for "primary property" that I prefer is:

"The intangible results of individual thinking life".

The thoughts of an individual that become ideas. This is

slightly changed from Galambos' definition, with gratitude to him for his definition. If mine is appropriate then it is to the credit of Galambos. If not, then the error is for my account.

Secondary property

Once a person has an idea and translates it into action the probable consequence is "secondary property". They create a tangible item. Anything from a sketch of "what might be" to a beautiful drawing, painting, or sculpture. Or a new clothing design or electronic product. A model airplane or doll for their child to play with.

One of the most incredible recent examples is from someone such as a J. K. Rowlings. Who—I think intending to write a story for a family member or friend—eventually enthralled millions of children. And adults.

Thinking of the previous definition for *primary property*, the definition of "secondary property" should be obvious:

"The tangible result of moral activities of individual life".

Again this is changed from Galambos' definition, with the same conditions applying. Concerning property, it should be pointed out that ownership of property is a moral concept. What do I mean by that?

That ownership can not be acquired through immoral action. If this were the case, then ownership could be acquired through theft. It would mean that I could steal something you owned and thereby become the owner myself. That all that would be required for the transfer of ownership would be to steal the desired item.

I do not think I need to point out that this would create a totally disorderly society. One whose main objective was to steal things. And as Galambos pointed out, you can not consume or steal something that does not exist. Something that has not yet been created. And there would be little incentive to create things, only to have them stolen.

You should also consider the fact that political states claim they own certain property. If this were so—that they own property rather than simply control it immorally—then this would be an application of the concept of "ownership through theft".

There are standard indications of ownership. Such as "title" to something, or a receipt indicating *moral* acquisition. But there are other indications of ownership also. A very basic one is that you can sell or rent that which you own. And that you are free to establish the price for such sale or rental. Recognizing that if the price is too high there will be no buyers. Too low and there will be many prospective buyers. But you may not maximize your income from the sale or rental.

This illustrates the bankruptcy of the concept of "public" property. That "the public" owns something such as Yellowstone National Park. Or the motorways, or "public" buildings. If I am actually an owner, I want to sell my property. I need the money. Also, I don't think some of "my" property is being properly taken care of by "my custodian". It may not be safe and properly maintained.

Control of property is another matter. That can and often is acquired through theft or other immoral action. Such as fraud and deception. From this we could create a usable definition of theft. Although perhaps not the most comprehensive.

First definition of theft:

"Control of property by someone other than the owner."

This does come close to another concept of "theft". That of the control of one person by another. Generally called "slavery". What is it when one person controls the body of another person? It is control of that property known as "primordial property".

This can also apply to primary and secondary property.

Slavery can be more than simply the control of a person's body. Of what they may or may not be able to do with their body. Such as the ability for "free movement". If someone controls the property other than the primordial property of a person—such as their house, car, access to telephone services, and water—this is also slavery.

It is important to note here that one person can never

completely control the *mind* of another individual. At least not without extreme measures, such as drugs that control the mind. In almost all other cases though the mind always has some ability to "free wheel". For uncontrolled thought.

Even in the infamous Gulag of Stalin where they certainly controlled almost all aspects of life there was still scope for largely unfettered thought. Witness the thinking of Solzhenitsyn and others.

It is clear that those who have been released from the American Gulag—Bush's infamous *Cages at Guantanamo*—that those there have retained some freedom of thought. It is also clear that many of them have been terrified during what is officially referred to as "interrogation". And are themselves thus the victims of terrorism, yes?

After all, what is terrorism? It is being terrified, yes? Is a "weapon of mass destruction" needed to do this? If a person thought they were being drowned by the question master might this not invoke a feeling of terror? Must more than one person be terrified for terrorism to have occurred? Ten, twenty? Or a politically-created consensus of 29.7 people?

Why don't we simplify the matter? And say that if one person has been terrified, then an act of terrorism has occurred? Then we don't need a "committee of experts" to verify that terrorism has occurred.

Morality

Now that we have defined property, we can define morality. Which also covers *ethics*, making ethics a very simple thing. It should be obvious that there can be only one "ethics". The concept of that action which is "ethical". That there is no need for so-called computer ethics, medical ethics, beekeeping ethics, business ethics, ethics for prostitutes and politicians, prison ethics and so on. And that *ethical* and *moral* are actually synonyms.

And when someone speaks of "the ethics of war" I almost experience a massive short-circuit in my brain. That is even worse than using the phrase "unlawful killing". Which implies there must be the opposite, yes? A "lawful killing". "Law", meaning unnatural or political law. That there is the concept that it might be okay to kill someone. Which of course it is not, again exposing the convoluted concept of politics for what it is: intellectual bankruptcy. To be kind.

We could define *moral* as…

> "Any action that does not *intentionally* degrade the qualify of life of another individual".

Thus in a sense a person can not really have "immoral thoughts". Thoughts are *amoral.* That is, having no morality content. You may laughingly think of blowing up Jones' house, to "wipe that smug expression off his face". But until you actually start to do it nothing immoral has happened. And such fantasies may persist from time-to-time as a relic of our current, primitive societal structure based on coercion.

We must emphasize the word "intentional" because *intent* does come into morality. Because if you accidentally interfere with the property of another person or otherwise degrade their quality of life, it is not a crime. But an accident. Which can often be rectified as we do now: with a simple apology.

Note that this concept of morality does not name any profession. That it is not exclusive to doctors or taxi drivers or businessmen. It applies to any and all human action.

At this point I would like to switch to a real-life situation that is much in the news. Often heralded as something like "... one of the most significant and important judicial situations and decisions of recent times". This is the most unfortunate situation of the two "Siamese" twins in England known as Mary and Jodie. Joined in such a way that separating them will result in one dying. And not separating them will almost certainly result in both dying.

The "High Court," the highest political court in England, ruled that they *must* be separated. As I told *Newsweek* magazine, I agree that this is the correct thing to do. But I also pointed out that it is okay for me to think this. But to impose the decision on the mother or father, the twins, or the medical staff would be totally immoral. The fact that I believe it is the only rational thing to do is and can be for my thoughts and account only. And not translated into a command or order.

The only individuals who can *morally* make the decision are the mother and father. It is they who have the "temporary moral custody" of the two lives. A contractual relationship that would normally end when the two beings had been properly prepared to make their own decisions concerning the conduct of their lives.

But until it has reached this point—morally and rationally—the parents are the *only* ones who can make this decision. Recognizing that one or more doctors must also decide if they would follow the wishes of the parents. And, again for myself, if I were the diagnostician and reached the conclusion that there was only one possible course of action—to operate now or they both will die—I would propose to operate if so requested by the parents.

To not operate would also be moral for a medical doctor. Especially if they had any reservations concerning the diagnosis or their surgical skills. Or if for any other reason they chose not to operate. But to require a doctor to operate is totally immoral. As is preventing a doctor from operating if they wished to do so and had parental approval. If they chose to operate *in spite of* the direction of the political court, rather than *because of it*, that is of course moral. Although in a political society it may not be rational for a slave to make such decisions.

Euthanasia

The preceding discussion and conclusions applies directly to the subject of euthanasia. The decision to die rests only with the person wishing to do so. Assuming they are mentally competent to do so.

Otherwise, the decision could rest with others who have been rationally and morally delegated to do so by the individual wishing to die when they were competence to make that decision.

And again, whether a physician wishes to assist or not is solely up to them. And any attempted or actual interference by *any* other party in this decision is immoral.

Rationality is another matter. But again, rationality is for the account of the person wishing to die. And any physician considering action in the matter. If they think it is irrational for the person to do it then they should not assist in that.

The incarceration of Dr. Jack Kevorkian in the USA is both immoral and irrational. The only criminals involved here are those who persecuted, sentenced and imprisoned him. And certainly not Dr. Kevorkian.

If he should die in prison, then those involved are—at the very least—accessories to murder.

Ethics and that act which is ethical (moral) is a very simple thing.

The concept of morality

Now that we have defined the basic operative words in the area of morality we may now discuss how to determine what is "right". And what this means.

What is *right*? What constitutes *rightness*? If you have been thinking you might reach the conclusion that it has something to do with that which is moral. That if something is moral it may also be "right". Which is true. But what is "true"?

It is not what Bureau Veritas or the "Truth Ministry" says is true. Or even—or especially—what a politician says acting for the political state says is true.

Before proceeding I decided to look in the dictionary. Not normally a repository of truth or semantic precision. To see what it said. As usual, I was not disappointed. I did not expect to find much of value, and did not. It has almost a quarter of a column of definitions for the word "true". Some of which are partially correct, most of which are redundant.

I think it best to return to the definition provided by Galambos. Which I believe to be the same as used by Newton and all those who achieve greatness in thinking:

True

"That which is observable."

Which means, "That which is observable using any or all of the five senses". The opposite being an operative definition of mysticism. As with all the steps leading to a conclusion based on this process, each step should be able to be corroborated by any other thinking being in the same situation and having the same intellectual capacity. In other words, if I see a friend being abducted by an alien, then many other people must be able to see and understand the same thing. Else it is not "true".

This is the first step in the gathering of data or information with which to create new and useful knowledge. *Observation.* To observe a phenomena or event and take notes regarding what you see, hear, smell, feel, or taste. But not that which "intuition" tells you that you observe. This comes later in extrapolating the data and forming new and different conclusions.

Usually when someone observes something they record more than one piece of data. They then begin to think about the meaning of what they have observed. To merge the thoughts with currently known and relevant information. And to "generalize" what they have learned and thought.

To create new knowledge there must be an extrapolation of current thinking on the subject. This may be as a result of something previously unobserved or incorrectly observed in the past by previous observers. Or, in both cases, there could have been an incorrect interpretation of the results.

To go though this process a person uses what is called "logical and valid thought processes". You must follow the accepted rules of logic that have long been used to create new and useful knowledge. And "valid" thought processes.

It also involves the concept of *discovery*. And the most elegant statement I know of to describe this is that of Albert

Szent-Gyürgyi von Nagryapolt.[7] When he said:

"Discovery consists in seeing what everyone else has seen, and thinking what no one else has thought."

I will not discuss this further, as the process is well known and there are many good references on the subject.

Except to say that you can easily identify major innovators. For, as Jonathan Swift said:

"When a true genius appears in the world,
you may know him by this sign,
that the dunces are all in a confederacy against him." [8]

It is this extrapolation of thought that creates new and useful knowledge. And also verifies the work of others who have done the same thing. This is called "corroboration". The extrapolation is that beautiful process of:

- Thinking what is.
- Thinking what could be as a result of what I have observed.

While we are at it I must define both *hypothesis* and *theory*. There is much confusion on this subject. To put it kindly.

Hypothesis

"A possible explanation for an event or phenomenon."

Theory

"The single, correct explanation for an event or phenomenon."

These definitions are mine, since I do not remember them from Galambos' lectures. Although I am certain that my definitions are influenced by his work. To the extent that they are correct, I would say they are his definitions or consistent with his definition. If incorrect, then that is for my account and not that of Galambos.

This is the same method that—since Newton—has been used to create new and useful knowledge in what is often

---

7 Albert Szent-Gyürgyi von Nagryapolt (1893-1986), Hungarian physicist and medical doctor. He won the Nobel Prize in Physiology and Medicine in 1937.

8 Jonathan Swift (1567-1745). *Thoughts on Various Subjects, Moral and Diverting*, 1728.

called "science". Or its result, technology.

But of course everyone looks at this and says, "... but that is *science*. And you can not use that concept for things involving *people*". Which of course is not true. And a major reason why our societal structure does not work. Has not worked for millennia. And can never work. There is no way to correct errors.

There is only one "small" addition that is needed to convert what is commonly called "The Scientific Method" to handle all aspects of volitional life. Non-technological as wall as technological knowledge. And, with credit to Galambos, that is the concept of morality and what is moral. The elucidation of this concept is one of the great achievements of Galambos.

If the results of implementing a theory are moral, then the action is said to be "right". *Right* on an absolute basis. Therefore also consistent with the laws of nature. Including the *Universal Laws of Volitional Behavior*. And we arrive at Galambos' definition of "rightness"

Rightness:

> "That which is based on true premises, valid and logical thought processes, and the resulting action does not *intentionally* interfere in the property of another person."

As I said, the recognition of adding the concept of that action which is *moral* to the results of the Scientific Method so that it can be used in "human action" is one of the great achievements of Galambos.

Chapter 3

The Actual Court

Now we have finally returned to that. In the process we have actually created the court. "What?! Created the court? What do you mean?"

Very simply, *any act sits in judgment on itself.* And of course the person who performs the act. Obviously, if I as an individual and not a minion of the state steal money it is a crime. It is "not right" by the process outlined above. It should also now be obvious that if I am a minion of the state—such as in the form of a tax collector—then I also stand convicted of theft in The Court of Planetary Justice

If I am either of the parents of Mary and Jodie and I elect to do nothing regarding the separation of the twins I am not guilty of a crime. But if the operation proceeds under the orders of the High Court, then those of the court who participated in the decision are guilty of a crime.

As is common in events involving politics and politicians, things can become very strange. If the doctors now refuse to obey the order, they could—in the eyes of the state—become criminals. It is a conundrum. If they do it—and it is against the wishes and desires of the parents—they are criminals according to natural law. But if they do not do it, then they are criminals according to unnatural law. According to political law.

The system of politics is one of false alternatives, convoluted thinking and twisted results. One of Galambos' favorite statements to indicate the criminality and absurdity of political action was to say the choice in principle is "would you rather have a broken arm or a broken leg". The rational individual wants neither. But that is not offered by the politician.

Many things that are legal are immoral. Many things that are moral are illegal. From what I have discussed above we can create a definition of *crime*. And of *justice*.

Crime

"Attempted and/or intentional interference in the property of another person."

Justice

"The condition that exists when all injustices are eliminated."

In a rational and moral society justice would be accepted and considered as a "given" and normal thing. So much so that it probably would not even be a concept. Just part of nature that you accept as the way nature is. Just as the concept of slavery would not be known.

Since the natural condition of thinking beings is to be free. To do anything that does not intentionally degrade the quality of life of another thinking being. And this condition would exist until some mutant misfit comes along and decides they will control the lives of others through force and fraud. And for some unfathomable reason, the victims accept this.

Recourse from injustice

Background

I had a hard time with a heading for this section. I did not wish to use the word "prosecution" because of its negative image.

Any justice system needs a method of handling injustices. Of events resulting from the commission of a crime. The basic problem with the current system is that it operates from—and is based on—a faulty concept. That it is acceptable to regulate a society of thinking beings using a coercive system. This is immoral and itself a criminal concept. As it requires interference in the property of others. Intentionally doing things that degrade the qualify of life of others.

And you must realize the such a system could not work for a large number of people and thousands of years were it not for the "hidden" and unspoken concept that disobedience of any unnatural law must be punishable by death. If not, the system would not work.

Please, you need to examine this truth. What must happen if you say you will not do what the ruler says. And you will not allow the ruler to fine you or to imprison you. Even if the "crime" is refusing to get a license for your dog or cat. That you refuse to do so, and that you will walk away from the political police who are saying "you must do this or else".

Think about it. And perhaps read:
<http://www.aristarchus.org/cat_nyt.php>.

And as for results, even the most die-hard believer in the system of politics should agree that it does not work. Even a huge organization of political police and a massive system of prisons—all operated at a very high monetary and social cost—has not stopped crime.

Further, there is almost never adequate recourse or compensation for the victims of crime. The fact that a thief goes to jail can not compensate a person for the loss of property. And that a murderer is executed is no compensation for the loss of life. And neither of these deter or prevent crime, yes?

What is needed is a system under which no one wishes to commit a crime. In which they "do not wish to be bothered with such distractions". It is not "profitable" to commit a crime. A system in which a person would much rather get on with making a better life for themselves in a moral and rational way than to commit an attack on the property of another person.

Then there is no crime.

But of course that might seem a bit "Utopian"? After all, no one is perfect. And people do experience a lapse in judgment from time-to-time. In this case the important thing is: how do you handle the exceptions, yes?

As Galambos would say "Show me a person who has never made a mistake and I will show you a person who has never done anything".

We should not think that no one will make a mistake, but how mistakes are handled. At the minimum cost to the individual and society, yet with proper compensation for the victims of mistakes.

Fortunately, the laws of nature tell us how to do this.

Specifically, Galambos' Laws, the *Universal Laws of Volitional Behavior.* And there is a mechanism currently in place to substitute for the judicial system, the vast penal system, the need for a large political police system, and the fact that victims are rarely compensated for a crime.

Chapter 4

The Laws of Nature

Galambos created what he referred to as the Laws of Volition. I have the temerity to rename these laws. To the "Universal Laws of Volitional Behavior". Galambos himself said his laws were universal in nature. And they do describe how nature regulates behavior. I also refer to them as *Galambos' Laws*. Which is moral and rational.

- **The first law of volitional behavior…**

  "Individual thinking beings seek to acquire the most amount of property for the least amount of effort".

  (If you have read other essays you will note that I have folded the first corollary into the first law.)

Were this not so, life as we know it could not exist. It is both a necessity for successful volitional life and something that is the cause of a great deal of mischief. This is the cause of people wishing to rule others, whether through force or fraud (mysticism). This basic law of nature will be familiar to readers of my essays.

Such readers will also know that—fortunately—there is a balancing,

Second law of volitional behavior…

"In the absence of coercion,
rational thinking beings seek happiness".

This does not seem like a very strong counterbalance to what appears to be motivation toward naked greed and unrestrained ambition. However, if you have read Chapter 11, "Need and Morality in Society" in my book *Cowardly New World* you will know that this can be a very effective deterrent to attempts to gain control of property through force or fraud.[9] In fact, it is *the* basis for the mechanism that replaces the current, primitive, regulatory mechanism of society: political laws and a political police to enforce them.[10]

Please note that the Second Law does not say an individual *will* find happiness in an action. More appropriate to political societies what it does say is that in the absence of coercion a rational-thinking individual will select an alternative that results in the *least unhappiness*. That given a choice a rational thinking person will not deliberately chose an unhappy outcome.

It also means the decision and perceived outcome is relative. It is relative to each individual and their description of happiness (or the least unhappiness) for them. Another individual with a different outlook on what makes them happy will chose a different action. It also says that any definition of happiness is valid (but that the action may not be moral or rational, and thus not necessarily right on an absolute basis) for any one individual. And that no other person should say that the definition of happiness of another individual is invalid. They may say it, but they may not impose that decision on them. So why waste time nitpicking?

To help understand this we should think about the subject of "goodness". Of that which is "good" for an individual. With there being absolute and subjective "goods".

Good (subjective)

"Any phenomena, process, or action that an individual prefers".

Good (absolute)

"Anything is an absolute good that is a subjective good to at least one person, but which does not involve the exercise of coercion".

Thinking about these two definitions should help to clarify things. Noting that the "absolute" good is a moral event? It takes place in society. In the interaction between two or

---

9 William W Morgan, *Cowardly New World: The Cause and Cure of Our Societal Problems*, Universal Salvage Corporation (Publisher), Escondido, USA (2006).

10 For more information on this, please read the essay on "False Alternatives and Human Destiny" in *Cowardly New World* above.

more thinking beings.

The search for individual happiness is the driver of all action. With the action being to acquire the most amount of property using the least amount of effort. With effort being the expenditure of intellectual and physical resources. What will tend to make this action moral is the search for happiness.

The parenthetical modifier above (related to an action that may not be rational) covers situations in which, for example, a person defends their property from attack by the state and is fined, imprisoned, or murdered as a result. This action may not seem rational to another person. Or indeed to the individual taking the course of action if they could relive the process and the results.

Psychologist might define the moment and action as "temporary insanity". But bear in mind that this was the result of coercion and extreme frustration brought on by the political state. Again illustrating how the concept of the political state attempts to contravene the Universal Laws of Volitional Behavior. And why the concept of politics and coercion as the basis for a societal structure has never worked. And never can work.

Please note that by property—as discussed earlier—I mean not only tangible property. But also intangible or "intellectual" property. And when the two laws of volitional behavior are merged it also explains why someone can enjoy a sunset, stroking a cat, or being stroked by another human being. The "property" known as tranquility—and perhaps other properties—may be acquired by these actions.

Chapter 5

The system of deterrence

Little deterrence would be required in a free society. One in which people could concentrate on making a better life for themselves and those for whom they have a direct responsibility.

When you wake up thinking that life is not so bad. And that the events of the day could make it even better, a person is not interested in doing something that would have a negative impact on this.

Today the majority of criminals are probably never even caught. And when they are, they plea bargain their way into a lesser sentence to relieve congestion in the system. Also, I think in a sense there are only three situations in which people commit crimes:

- They think that given the faulty justice and police systems they can get it away with it.
- There is some mental aberration, with a possible physiological basis.
- They are frustrated to the point of irrationality.

There is another thing also. When people are constantly told what they may and may not do they may begin to want to challenge the system.

They may also be forced into the situation of an engineer involved in the building of the Titanic. He observed there were not enough life boats. And reported this to management. He was told that "it satisfies government regulations" and that he should say nothing further about it. Both the action of telling him to do this and his acquiescence were immoral. Politics creates this type of situation very often.

In the absence of a physiological cause, virtually no one who feels yesterday was good and tomorrow may be better commits a crime. Especially if there is the thought they may not get away with it.

So what type of system would create this situation?

Chapter 6

Credit and Restitution

Yes, our current credit system slightly modified. And the fact that in a rational and durable societal system based on individual freedom all property has an owner. I should not need to modify that by saying a "moral owner". One who acquired the property morally.

The recognition of the fact that the normal credit mechanism can be the moral regulatory system of behavior in a free society is another of the great intellectual achievements of Galambos.

The fact that no one likes a criminal. And would prefer not to associate with them or do business with them.

Anyone believing that someone had committed a crime—interference in the property of another person—might not wish to do business with that person. This is a perfectly moral decision. Only in coercive political societies is a person required to deal with a person "... regardless of race, creed and color". Or immoral behavior.

When I was a child many shops had signs stating "We reserve the right to refuse service to anyone". This is moral. But may not always be rational. Especially when in the past in America it was based on the fact that some people did not wish to serve Blacks, Mexicans, Asians, and assorted other people. Or perhaps even Jews, Catholics, Protestants, Muslims or whatever.

This is not completely rational as it limits a person's market. But it is moral.

You hear that someone you know or heard about has committed a crime. You own a petrol station, food market, telephone company, water company or you provide some product or service. It is moral to refuse to serve that person.

When other suppliers of goods and services do the same life might become difficult for the person. So difficult that they might regret having done what they did. And like to try to reverse the situation or "get out of it".

It is a bit like the old English concept of "sending a person to Coventry". Do not talk to them, have nothing to do with them. They become a non-person.

What can be done? How do they get out of it? And have their electricity, water and telephone service restored. Be able to purchase food. Go to the cinema.

The restitution system

All that is needed is for the person to realize they have made a mistake, and to then:

- Offer an apology.
- Offer restitution for their crime.

It is up to the person against whom the crime has been committed—the victim of the crime—whether they accept the apology and the restitution. However, as long as the proposed restitution is somewhat "reasonable" it might be irrational to not accept it. And to let all parties get on with their lives. A history of not accepting what to others seemed reasonable could actually damage the credit rating of the person who did not accept restitution "under any circumstances".

Restoration of credit

Once restitution has been accepted and published then it is up to the market to determine how quickly and to what degree credit is restored. But again common sense would probably rule as it does today.

Restoration of credit does not necessarily mean that everyone will be "good friends" with the reformed one. It merely means they would trade with them. As today, anything more would be an evolving, personal matter for those concerned.

False accusations

What about the problem of false accusations? Would it not be possible that someone could be falsely accused of a property transgression? Yes, of course. If so, then the tables are turned. The accused could actually refuse "credit" or not grant trading privileges to those who falsely accused them. And encourage others to do the same. Again, this is little different than today.

The role of the clearing house

The concept of the clearing house is probably much more pervasive and common than most people realize.

Many people are familiar with the general activities of a bank clearing house. And most probably feel that is the only type of clearing house there is.

But a credit agency also functions as a clearing house. And in a free world the clearing house would have enormous importance and significance. You might even say it would be the "conscience of a society". And would also have its own credit rating. To the extent that it did its job morally and rationally, it would have a good credit rating.

If it made few mistakes at "certifying" that a crime had taken place, and was good at creating solutions acceptable to the market, it would have a high credit rating.

Although a thought just occurred to me. As related to crime, the credit agency business would be a dying industry. As a rational and durable society matured, crime would disappear.

The credit bureau would become like the Maytag service man in their one-time advertisements. The telephone covered with cobwebs. The lone employee sleeping. As the phone rings for the first time in a century to report an act of intentional property interference...

Chapter 7

The planetary court of justice, revisited

I think we have just defined a planetary court of justice. What do you think?

I think it would be society and the summation of all credit bureaus, and their resulting activity.

They would be:

- An investigative agency.
- A credit rating agency.
- A conflict resolution agency.

In a sense it also functions as the:

- Prison system.
- The parole system.
- Credit restoration system.

Although for the latter, it is largely the "criminal" who does the restoring. The credit bureau merely notes and publicizes the information as appropriate. It may also function as an "arbitration" agency between the property transgressor and the victim.

Please notice that there is no "enforcement" police system. This is a self-policing system. As you would expect in a truly free society.

And as I indicated above, this would almost certainly be functional only during the transition from a society based on coercion to one of total individual freedom.

The Judge and Jury

All court systems require a judge and jury, yes? From the preceding it appears to me that the cast would consist of:

Judge.............................. : The "concept of rightness".
Prosecution.................. : Truth, Validity
Jury .... : The market, facilitated by the clearing house concept.

Summary

Does anyone believe that the current "justice" system works? That there is justice for either accused or victim?

Do you believe that most criminals are caught? Is "most" enough? Or should it be *all* criminals? Do you believe that any criminals go unpunished? Or that some people who are innocent are incorrectly accused and sentenced? Sometimes even to death?

Is the death penalty an answer to anything? Is there restitution to victims?

Answers will vary for many reasons.

What has been presented has never been tried in its entirety. But it is consistent with the laws of nature. Especially those laws related to how people behave in the absence of coercion. Which is the ideal system. Not only that, it is the only workable system.

It is a self-policing and self-correcting system. These do not work in a coercive society. For reasons that should now be obvious.

Chapter 8

The Court is Now in Session

All the accused should now become obvious. They will automatically "appear before the court" whenever they wish to purchase a product or service.

And be sentenced accordingly.

And we should get on with building a rational and durable society whose time-scale of existence will be concomitant with that of our local universe. And with greater knowledge, perhaps with other universes.

Getting rid of the "distractions" caused by politics will also allow us to solve the problems related to global warming. Which we will *not* be able to solve until we do so.

The reason I put "distractions" in quotation marks is because the products of politics are more than distractions, yes? The dysfunctional healthcare, school and pensions systems. Lack of freedom and security. War, famine, hunger, malnutrition and all the other things you see on the daily news.

You can visit the publisher web site and may be able to vote on the credit rating of some of the major criminals of our time. The address:

<http://universal-salveage.org.uk/pcoj/>

Chapter 9

The Crimes

We are surrounded by crime. We live in a sea of it. Almost drowning in it. After all, our very societal system is a crime, yes? Requiring that one or a few people control the lives and property of all others. And in the 5,000 years or so of recorded history we know this has not worked. Not one societal problem solved.

In addition to "general" or "private" crime, there is the crime of the activities of politicians, operating in the underworld of politics. And in fact this forms by far the largest number of criminal actions. With our current population, billions of crimes every day. As part of routine daily life.

But then there have been the spectacular crimes by political rulers. Such as Alexander, the Roman emperors, Genghis Khan and his successors. The kings and popes of Europe. And especially Urban II, the creator of the first great Jihad in history. Ironically, by a Christian, yes? The one that started the roughly 900 year war (1100 to now) between Christians and Muslims.

Then of course Napoleon, Hitler and Stalin. The British and French politicians and bureaucrats who meddled in the Middle East for several hundred years from about 1700-1950, ensuring that terrorism would fester and grow. Followed by the Americans.

Hitler and his buffoon-friend Mussolini, with the starting of the Second World War. Ably assisted by the Japanese. And we have a conflagration that killed at least 50 *million* people.

The Chinese under Mao and the North Koreans under Kim Il Sung got involved and probably another few million died. Then the criminal activities of Kennedy and Johnson. Another 3-5 million dead.

Millions have died in the Congo under Mobutu. And tens of millions in all of Africa.

Lest you think I am mean and uncaring of Americans, American history and politicians, I will tell you a personal story. Forty years ago or so I cried when Kennedy was assassinated. Cried for days.

I was in the town of Hof, Germany. Which then was inside the 5 km buffer zone of the border separating West and East Germany. In a small coffee shop. Idly listening to some music on the radio. When the announcer said: "Wir unterbrechen dieses Programm: John F. Kennedy, der fünf und dreiziger President der Vereinigte Staaten ist tot".[11]

A hush fell over the place. I thought I did not understand properly. Yet from the eyes of those around me I knew it must be true.

My German wife did not understand my grief. I was thinking of many things. The death of youth? The noble objectives of the Pease Corps? Of innocence? The image of Kennedy with little John-John, smiling at each other. Then, later, the little boy saluting his dead father.

The only time I ever engaged in political voting in my life—it being a criminal offense—I had voted for Nixon.[12] But then when I saw the young and handsome Kennedy taking the oath of office, and the things he said, I was sorry I had voted for Nixon. And glad Kennedy had won.

I have learned slowly. Now decades later I know there can be no solution to our societal problems through coercion. Yet I can still grieve for the loss of life. He was not *trying* to do bad. And death is the ultimate disaster for any thinking being. Even the worst do not need that. It is still immoral to take the life of another person unless they personally—personally between you and that person—attack you. And it is reasonably certain you will be killed if you do not kill the other person.

---

11 I apologize if I do not remember the German correctly…

12 You are not only voting for people to control your own life and property, but also to control that of many others. To force them to do things, prevent them from doing things. Maybe to destroy hopes and dreams for their life.

Self defense is always moral. Although perhaps not always rational. If you can disable the other person without killing them, that is the better result. But unless a person is expert in those things, it may be best to not take a chance when it is apparent you will die if you do not with certainty disable the attacker.

A few days ago (about January 30th, 2007) I just read something I could not believe. Even from the theatre of the absurd and barbaric: politics. An American senator no less, discussing the Iraq crime against humanity of Bush. Saying "we"—the Americans whose lives he controls—should not give up in Iraq. Not make the same mistake as in Vietnam. "When we were actually winning until a weak 'administration' gave in and did not send yet more troops". That is paraphrased, but reasonably accurate.

How could anyone be so ignorant and deluded?! What does he mean by "winning"? Killing another few million people? And does he really believe America could have "won"? Meaning subdued the Vietnamese? He does not know history. No one has done that. Not in a thousand years.

Even the mighty Kublai Kahn lost his entire fleet of 350 ships and 50,000 warriors. The Chinese lost many times, or were simply assimilated and disappeared. The French lost twice, the Japanese once. This irrationality is in addition to the issue of immorality.

If American rulers had had the ignorance and tenacity to continue, the war would probably still be going on. And now it would be 200,000 or so Americans and 5-7 million Vietnamese dead? Again, for what?

Look at Vietnam now. It is more of a capitalist country than the US. Most Vietnamese—which is those under about 25 or so—almost adore all things American. Unbelievably. There is no animosity. They are not taught in school that Americans were or are bad. And they buy billions of dollars of goods from America every year. Employing tens of thousands of Americans. So strange is our perverse, barbaric and bizarre world…

History books actually glorify Napoleon, yes? Yet he killed millions of people. Destroyed a vast amount of property. Impoverished France and Europe for a century. This is "wonderful and glorious"? Worthy of many pages in the encyclopedia? Hundreds of history books? You only need one single, simple entry. His name and dates. And the notation "serial killer on a massive scale".

The Sentence and Punishment

It should be the same for all. No executions, and no incarceration in a "brick and mortar" prison. Rather, the maximum sentence of ensuring they understand they have no importance or significance in history. They have become totally irrelevant in history and in society. And have been "sent to Coventry". There will be no one who wishes to talk to them. With no access to the police powers—including military—of a political entity they represent a danger to no one.

When each criminal and their crime is discussed following, it should be assumed that the above should be their sentence if convicted by the court. Even though nothing is said about the sentence.

But in some cases there may be hope for the future. If the crime is not so egregious, there were no obvious bad intentions, and they confess their ignorance, then there may be hope for rehabilitation. It depends only on market acceptance of this plea.

Other events

What about the kidnapping, rendition and torture of Hassan Mustafa Osama Nasr, also known as Abu Omar? As an example case.

Flights into and over the air space of another country require a "Dip Clear". Diplomatic clearance. Flight details must be provided. It is certain that false statements were made. Else the flights would almost certainly never have been approved. If no false statements were made, then officials of the concerned countries are guilty of the relevant crimes. Of conspiracy in aiding and abetting the commission of a crime.

Such a thing would require the complicity of the US Department of State. And for something as "sensitive" as this, the explicit knowledge and approval of the Secretary. It would almost certainly require the approval and knowledge of the National Security Advisor.

And in the Bush Régime, none of these individuals would have had the temerity to take the actions on their own initiative. Without the explicit approval of the head of the régime. And as close as they are, it is very doubtful that the Deputy Ruler did not know of this, yes?

Therefore, in addition to any other crimes, there has been that cherished political crime: "conspiracy".

And perhaps the ruler and deputy ruler should suffer the same fate as Nixon? Who was guilty of far less heinous crimes. And the other conspirators should suffer market justice. And America could start with a clean slate with the Speaker of the House replacing the top criminals.

The troubles of Clinton seem almost laughable. The possibility of not telling the truth on some matter that did not imperil the world or kill hundreds of thousands? Compare this to semantic activities of Bush. And the death of hundreds of thousand of people who would not have died.

A president who had his mind on things other than revenge and killing people is a much more worthy individual. Lying is a common, every day, routine matter in politics. How hypocritical of politicians to persecute one of their own for this.

Many people have died as result of the rule of many tyrants.

George W. Bush

He is supposedly the great *Justice Giver*. Bringing justice to the oppressed peoples of the world. Such as in Afghanistan and Iraq, yes? Perhaps soon in Iran. The "world's policemen".

He said that:

"Under Saddam's regime many hundreds of thousands of people have died as a result of his actions - the vast majority of them Muslims"[13]

This from the web site of US White House: <http://www.whitehouse.gov/news/releases/2003/04/20030404-1.html>.

How many people died under the Bush régime? Not only did he engineer the death of more than the 3,000 Americans, but it is estimated that at least several hundred thousand people—and perhaps up to a million—have died in Iraq *as a direct result of actions by Bush.* Plus those who have died in Afghanistan. Well? They would not have died would they, if Bush had not used what now appears to have been his "private militia" to attack Iraq. Approved by his equivalent of a "Revolutionary Command Council" (RCC). Is there any difference in *principle* between the RCC and the US Congress? Advisors to the Ruler doing as he "suggests". Cheering and applauding him, as the RCC did Hussein. And the rubber-stamp cabinet was no different than a rubber-stamp politburo.

Anyone with any understanding of history should have known of the cause of modern terrorism. And the solution to this. As explained in my book *On…Terrorism: Simple Cause—Simple Cure.*[14] And that an attack on the Muslim world—such as Afghanistan and Iraq—would inflame the situation rather than solve the problem. Which is what happened, yes?

No only did many die in Afghanistan as a result of Bush's invasion—and he should not get the sole discredit for this—but there were many who died in other ways. Such as those he starved to death because Bush demanded that Pakistan not allow truck conveys to take food to Afghanistan. Food that would normally and routinely be delivered, but even food provided by international relief agencies.

Bush's invasion of Afghanistan was little different than that of the Russians. No true, actually. Bush had access to

---

13 Operation Iraqi Freedom, *Life Under Saddam Hussein.* < http://www.whitehouse.gov/news/releases/2003/04/20030404-1.html>

14 William W Morgan, *On… Terrorism: Simple Cause—Simple Cure*, Universal Salvage, Escondido, USA (2007).

much more devastating weapons. And more of them. The so-called "daisy cutters" and cluster bombs. Cruise missiles and Predator drones. A chance to try out new weapons before his planned attack on the people of Iraq.

Besides the deaths in Afghanistan, as it would be in Iraq later, millions were left homeless and starving.

"By late October, aid officials estimated that over a million had fled their homes, including 80% of the population of Jalalabad, only a 'tiny fraction' able to cross the border, most scattering to the countryside where there was little food or shelter or possibility of delivering aid; appeals from aid agencies to suspend attacks to allow delivery of supplies were again rejected by Blair, ignored by the U.S." [15]

So now we have Mr. Blair also. Who will be dealt with separately.

How many died in Afghanistan in addition to those who died in Iraq? Ask Mr. Bush. He is usually good with statistics, yes? If he does not supply the information, then the prosecution can find it. The "prosecution" being all those Homo sapiens (thinking beings...) who wish to know what he did that might effect his credit rating.

This in spite of a UN that he likes to use when it suits him, but ignores when it doesn't. While chastising those who seek to follow in his footsteps. And in spite of world opinion. Is doing as he wishes and "penning exceptions" any different than the "ruling by decree" that he is ostensibly against?

---

15 "Supplies of food `not getting through to refugees'," FT, Oct. 22; Edward Luce, "Aid agencies troubled as Afghans disperse," FT, Oct. 23; Elizabeth Becker, "U.N. Plans Relief Airlifts," NYT, Oct. 23; also an upbeat report by Jane Perlez, blaming the Taliban, same day. Aid agencies reported that "Taliban officials were helping British food and medical aid reach tens of thousands of Afghan refugees in desperate condition"; Mark Nicholson, Michela Wrong, Guy Dinmore, "UN warns of threat to relief in hostile areas," FT, Oct. 11. On condemnation by aid agencies of "inaccurate propaganda" by the U.S.-British "spin-machine" seeking to deflect responsibility for the "expected humanitarian crisis" to the Taliban, see Jo Dillon, Independent, Dec. 9, 2001.

It is not normal "Western" democracy, but Bush democracy. The same type he has brought to Iraq. That in which he has the final word, and not the people. In January and February 2007 is he not disregarding the will of the people?

Although as you should know, democracy is a failed concept. It and individual freedom are mutually exclusive concepts.

I recommend reading "The War in Afghanistan", by Noam Chomsky. As excerpted from Lakawala lecture, New Delhi. You can read it on-line at:
<http://www.zmag.org/lakdawalalec.htm>

You can also read more on the Bush régime's duplicity in Afghanistan and Iraq at:
<http://www.dissidentvoice.org/Aug05/Leupp0824.htm>

In the above article you can see that *Dour Leade*r is responsible for the murder attempt in Afghanistan of someone who had no connection with 9-11. A man named Hekmatyar. Someone with a long history of cooperation with the US political régime. He was targeted by one of the CIA's Predator spy planes.[16]

There you will also see that an American official—later an ambassador to Iraq—entertained Taliban officials in Afghanistan.

You should know and must remember that the Taliban was not anti-US. Maybe in words, but not in action. Osama bin Laden returned to Afghanistan, but *not* by invitation of Mullah Omar. And whatever you may think of the Taliban, they had severely limited the growing and harvesting of poppies. And were no more puritanical and oppressive than some of the régimes now and previously supported by Bush.

In a recent news report (January 2007), I read that "a White House spokesman" says that Bush "grieves for each one that is lost" and "would ensure that their sacrifices were

---

16 New reports indicate Bush failed in his attempt to murder the former associate. But he tried. And there must have been some "collateral damage"? The wrong person or persons murdered?

not made in vain". To be unnecessarily kind, this is poppycock. It almost smacks of attempted "restitution" for Bush's crimes. How can he possibly "ensure their sacrifice was not in vain"? What does it mean? First, they did not make a sacrifice. They were duped into going to war so Bush could gain revenge. Merely the old "eye for an eye" concept, using the American military as a private militia.

The plain fact is that none of the hundreds of thousand of Iraqis would have died were it not for the actions of Bush. What does that say about where the irresponsibility lies?

No result can ever pay for the loss of a human life. The only result that could is to make sure the individual did not die in the first place. Or if they did, that life was restored to them. This is beyond our current biological knowledge.

There are estimates of $1 *trillion* for the cost of *Bush's Blunder*. That's for the Americans. For the Iraqis it has devastated their economy. Millions are homeless. More millions are living as exiles in Jordan and Syria.

At $20,000 per year of income, that represents 5 million slave years for Americans. Or 1 million people slaves for 5 years. Or 125,000 people slaves for an entire lifetime. But since they need something for housing and food, it would be somewhat more people working as slaves for *Bush's Blunder*.

Think of the diseases that might be cured with a $1 trillion investment? The improvement that might be made in schools. It might even be possible for some of them to educate people. Who might not vote to "follow the leader" the next time.

Bush swore an oath to defend and support the constitution. The preamble to which says… "… establish justice insure domestic tranquility… promote the general welfare…".

When more than half of the people are against him and his actions he has not been promoting "domestic tranquility", yes? He has effectively said "I will do what I want, not what you want". Remembering that in the hallowed elections a majority of the people said they did not want what he said they must have. He is not acting consistent with the oath.

He has willfully, intentionally ("Pre-emptive strikes" and "Stay the course...") destroyed the image of America and American influence in the Middle East and much of the world. Bringing "comfort to the enemies of America". What does constitutional law call such a person?

Those in Guantanamo are deemed "enemy combatants". If they should be found guilty it would have been of killing tens or maybe a few thousand people. Bush has killed hundreds of thousands of people. More than Saddam killed in his 1987-1988 campaign against the Kurds.

Bush would also be deemed an "enemy combatant" by those from other countries whose citizens he has killed. There is question of the guilt of the people at Guantanamo. But no question of the guilt of Bush. Under the doctrine of "equal justice", so important to Americans, should Bush not (and of course his sidekick Cheney also) be subject to trial by a military tribunal?

He controls only 5% of the world population directly. So for those on whom he uses terror tactics in the other 95% of the world—to make things equal, a "level playing field" as he likes to promote—he would be the "enemy combatant", yes? And again for equality sake and in the interest of the democratic principles he promotes, he should be dealt with under the same rules he promotes for others, yes?

George W. Bush is not a proper successor to George Washington. Who, after helpless continental soldier's were murdered by British soldiers at the Battle of Princeton, told his own soldiers after they had captured some British troops and his men wanted to exact revenge: "Treat them with humanity, and let them have no reason to complain of our copying the brutal example of the British army in their treatment of our unfortunate brethren".[17]

Further, as a general thing, Washington often reminded his troops that "...they were an army of liberty and freedom, and that the rights of humanity for which they were fighting

---

[17] From *Washington's Crossing*, by David Hackett Fischer.

should extend even to their enemies".[18]

This was Washington's attitude toward mercenaries. Who today would probably be referred to as "enemy combatants" and "terrorists", yes?

Does this describe the actions of Washington's successor? Is he a worthy successor?

Think of the contract with your "political agent". Who violates your wishes and you then have no recourse. Violating the concept of contract law. The insolence of having "closed door hearings" and secrets that are kept from you, the enabler. The individual from whom their very power springs. You have created a monster that now controls *you*, the source of *their* power.

Even though George W. Bush has no understanding of American history, no respect for the concept of the founder of America and obvious disregard for the constitution, he should still receive justice. In the sense of that which is moral and rational for a free society. And only be "sent to Coventry" as his sentence.

It is interesting that of all the political presidents that America has had, that George W Bush has the lowest IQ of all. And IQ of 91, as indicated by the report of the Lowenstein Institute.[19] For confirmation that people who descend to the position where they can control the lives of others are usually the least fit, please read the statement of Thomas Paine:

---

18 Ibid.

19 <http://www.lovenstein.org/report/>.

"Men who look upon themselves born to reign, and others to obey, soon grow insolent; selected from the rest of mankind their minds are early poisoned by importance; and the world they act in differs so materially from the world at large, that they have but little opportunity of knowing its true interests, and when they succeed to the government are frequently the most ignorant and unfit of any throughout the dominions."[20]

Please remember that Thomas Paine is America's "godfather". Assuming Washington was the "father". As it was Paine's pamphlet *Common Sense*, published on January 10th, 1776 that created the sentiment and movement for independence from Britain. And then Paine who was actually the author of the Declaration of Independence.

Also interesting, is that the only other president below 100 is his father. Both of whom could have averted the *9-11* attack and stopped modern terrorism in its tracks if they had understood history and what motivates people to engage in what we refer to as "terrorism".

For confirmation on this please refer to my book *On... Terrorism: Simple Cause—Simple Cure.*[21]

Leonid Brezhnev

Brezhnev's largest toll on the life of others was as a result of the "Prague Spring" and the start of the War in Afghanistan. It started during his régime, but he died about three years into it. You could say that as the one in charge when the war started, he was the cause of death for all those who died.

The millions left homeless. The vast amount of property destroyed. The millions of hopes and dreams of individual life.

---

20 Thomas Paine, *Common Sense* (1776).

21 William W Morgan, On... Terrorism: Simple Cause—Simple Cure, Universal Salvage, USA (2007). <http://universal-salvage.org.uk/book_list.php#on>.

General George W. Casey, Jr.

Is he really any different than SS Obergruppen Führer Sepp Dietrich? Whose main quality was devotion to his Führer. For which, after 3,000 Americans and tens of thousands of Iraqis have died; the Iraqi economy is in tatters, with millions of them homeless and other millions exiles in neighboring countries; more than $1 trillion dollars is gone, with billions literally disappearing; he will be promoted to run the entire US Army.

And when questioned by a US Senate panel about his performance and the situation, Casey said ""I actually don't see it as a slow failure; I see it as slow progress".[22]

Why is it that when individuals descend into the realm of politics—whether it is the civil, military or religious branch—any semblance of intelligence disappears? They become permanently disconnected from reality? And are incapable of acting morally and rationally.

And for this show of absolute loyalty to the *Führer*, Gen Casey is being promoted to a higher level of incompetence.

The Senate and other politicians may vote on this matter. But I think the most important vote started some time ago. That of the Homo sapiens of this planet. In the Planetary Court of Justice.

Bush needs to understand that, while he can continue to play at making decisions, there is really only one decision maker. And it is those who empower him that make the supposedly "final" decision, yes? That is the principle of the system he cherishes, democracy.

And that decision was made some time ago. Concerning both his previous "preliminary decisions", and his legacy. The final decision. And that decision has been that his legacy will be one of irrelevancy in history. People not only do not want the "books" of his presidency, they don't even want the library itself.

---

22 <http://www.nytimes.com/2007/02/02/washington/02general.html?th&emc=th>.

In February 2007 nearly 10,000 people signed a petition against having his "Presidential Library" at SMU.[23] Earlier, a staff editorial at Baylor said that the "Consequences of Bush Library outweigh benefits".[24]

If *Dour Leader* should be foolish enough to attack Iran, would you want Gen Casey as the top Army man? With the same result as in Iraq? Although perhaps we should not blame him too much? He was only showing respect for "The Leader" and following orders, yes?

Tony Blair

The de facto ruler of what was once Great Britain, but now just Britain. A result of them being forced out of their position of ruling oil-producing countries in the Middle East. And forced to become an American puppet regime. Styled as a "special relationship" by Blair, but thought of with a bit of derision by those of the Bush régime. At least after Margaret Thatcher, who was her own person. Having only a friendship with the then-American ruler and definitely not his toady.

The British should have known better than to get involved in yet another adventure in the Middle East. After having been thrown out of India, Rhodesia, Egypt, Jordan, Iran, Oman, Bahrain and other places in the Middle East, Near East and Africa. Many of the British politicians of the past could have told Blair about the existence and power of the tribal societies in the Middle East.

But now Blair shares with George W. Bush the responsibility for the death of what is almost certainly millions of people. What percentage? Is that really important? Even the intentional killing of one person is murder. If you are an "ordinary" person you do not get a lesser sentence because you murdered less than 100,000 people, yes? Why should an "ordinary working man" be suddenly absolved of the possibility of murder charges simply because he is now a politician?

23 <http://www.wfn.org/2007/02/msg00044.html>.

24 <http://www.baylor.edu/Lariat/news.php?action=story&story=43750>.

Which seems to be the case in democracies, yes? Although politicians execute people who do that when they have the appellation of "dictator" rather than "prime minister", yes? Whey the discrimination? The US prohibits "bias" and "discrimination" in the workplace. And this is the politicians workplace. What about the hallowed "level playing" field?

As Voltaire said:

"It is forbidden to kill; therefore all murderers are punished unless they kill in large numbers and to the sound of trumpets."[25]

If a majority of the people in my neighborhood voted that I go kill a man in another country, if I were caught I would be tried and probably executed, yes? But if I am anointed "politician", and my "neighborhood" is now my country and I want to go off and kill someone in another country I can do that, yes? I only need to refer to it as a "war". Even "police action" or "régime change" might do. And as we know, certainly if I accuse my nemesis of "terrorism". Then I can use terrifying "shock and awe" tactics, yes?

Why a generalized diversion like this for Blair and not for Bush? I don't know. It just came to mind. But it applies to all tyrants, democratic or otherwise.

And, as with his mentor, who led him willingly to disaster, not even his people want him. They want him to step up from the position to which he descended ten years ago.[26]

And now, even more out of sequence. I am angry, as you should be. What about General Pinochet? He was accused of murdering people. His own people. But probably "only" about 1% as many as Bush and his cohorts murdered. Yet there was a huge outcry for trying Pinochet. Many attempts were made, but because of his age and other factors he slipped away.

But then he should have been reviled, yes? As he was a

---

25 Francoise Marie Arouet [Voltaire] (1694-1778).

26 We must remember that when politicians "assume power", they step down to position that not only allows but requires the exercise of immorality. And thus when they leave office, they "step up". To a position where if they commit murder they can be prosecuted for it.

"dictator". Not the ruler of a democracy such as Bush and Blair. People in that class must have special immunity, yes? Or is it because it is okay to punish those whose native language is not English? Or who have a different skin color? Who are not "one of us"? And obviously do not have "equal rights". Or equal moral obligations?

Maybe to create a "level playing field" we should eliminate the concept of politics? Of societies based on coercion? Then there would be *no one* that is immune from prosecution for large scale crimes. Better, there would be no one who wanted to or could commit such large scale crimes. Without coercion how would you "raise an army"?

If you had a good job—job security—would you give it up just because someone wanted you to go off and kill other people?

Please think about this...

Aznar, Howard and others

These are bit players. Although also deserving of discredit. Again, it makes no difference whether your immoral and irrational action kills one or more than one. Remembering there is an inverse relationship between *legality* and *morality*. That which is legal is a very relative and flexible concept. What is *legal* is what a particular political régime defines as being "legal".

The fact that what one régime may state is illegal is legal in a different régime should give pause. Maybe it is not an absolute concept? As corroborated by Bush and his "penning" of new laws. He is making political laws on the spot, yes? This is truly "democracy in action". Instant action. With a certain "folksy" casualness. I wonder if Saddam Hussein ever knew that Bush was quietly dictating...?

I have long objected to the idea that someone should claim *responsibility* for a bombing or attack on life. As when there is a bombing the news media and others wait for someone to "claim *responsibility*". I maintain they should be claiming *irresponsibility*.

Responsibility is a positive concept. Irresponsibility a negative one. Such as "I was acting *irresponsibly* when I spilled the hot coffee on you. I was not taking proper care and consideration to what I was doing. I was not acting *responsibly*".

By not thinking about what they were doing—really thinking—Aznar, Blair, Bush, Howard and others acted irresponsibly. But since they acted *intentionally*—with malice aforethought—they are *responsible* for what they did. Is deliberately going out and attacking another thinking being a rational act? One characteristic of a thinking specie? Is the endless cycle of killing and taking revenge worthy of a thinking specie?

And a "pre-emptive" strike might be synonymous with "premeditated", yes? Which usually ensures a more severe sentence, yes? If we follow the rules of politics I should be able to heed the call of my neighbors (a majority, mind you…) and go murder someone? If questioned I need only say it was a "pre-emptive strike". And if I added that "a majority" approve the act. And really seal the matter by saying I had consulted God before taking the action.

I will say yet again, defense of *your own* property is always moral. Although perhaps not rational. But you must remember that it is *morality* which is a societal concept. And *not* rationality. And that it is much more the morality content of our actions that will determine our survival as a specie than the rationality content. Because we consciously strive for rationality. Knowing clearly that it is in our own individual self-interest to have a good outcome on an action.

Isn't it better to try to do those things that make your own life better but also that you do not *intentionally* degrade the quality of life of another person? Then there is much less chance someone will want to interfere with your life. Why should they?

Maybe the preceding should go in a "summary" section. But I started it here and will leave it here. It has importance beyond its location…

Lyndon Johnson

He more than others is associated with the American War in Vietnam. Which the Americans refer to as the Vietnam War. Yes, there was a Vietnam War going on also. The one between the North and the South. But this would not have killed 3-5 million Vietnamese people and almost 60,000 Americans where it not for the American intervention in a civil war.

Johnson was nearly 40% more intelligent than George W Bush. So maybe the problem is the system that allows this, more than the individual…?

And while both Kennedy and Nixon where involved in it, they perhaps have less irresponsibility. Even when it was Kennedy who started it. It is possible Kennedy might have stopped it had he lived. Not that this makes it moral. Or even less immoral. Simply that fewer people would have died.

And Kennedy was nearly 40% more intelligent than Johnson. Were it not for the anomaly of Bush, we might even say that intelligence was a bad thing for political presidents? But rather than speculate on such things, why don't we eliminate the situation in which one person is allowed to control the lives of others? Eliminate mass slavery.

Besides being emotional about the "Communist problem", Johnson was also abysmally ignorant of history. Especially the fact that no attacker of Vietnam has been successful in more than a thousand years. Even the "great" Kublai Khan experienced a humiliating, almost instant defeat. With the loss in about a day of perhaps 350 ships and 50,000 men. Wisely, he did not decide to "stay the course".

Many people now vilify Johnson. As they should. The Americans are still searching for something less than 2,000 "missing in action" people. One figure says the Vietnamese may have 300,000 or so that are missing and not accounted for. And they did not start the war that resulted in the death of millions of Vietnamese and almost 60,000 Americans.

Plus there have been tens of thousands of people who have died or suffered devastating defects from the "Agent

Orange" defoliant that was sprayed on the jungles in a vain attempt to find and close the Ho Chi Minh Trail.

Every investigator from every country other than the US has said the Agent Orange was responsible for the horrific and relatively very large number of birth defects occurring in the areas where Agent Orange was sprayed. Except for "investigators" from the US of course. A bit like Bush's "official investigators" into the causes of global warming?

And everyone now knows that Americans committed "war crimes" in Vietnam. The My Lai Massacre and other such things. As there have been in Iraq.

Yet the fact that one person can effectively declare and continue war is also a "crime against humanity". The taking of one single human life is a "crime against humanity". It does not require more than one.

You should also read my definition of *Crime Against Humanity*. Which I will repeat here:

"The societal condition that exists when one individual is allowed to interfere in the property of another or the act of doing so."

The societal system of democracy allows this. Something you should please think about…?

And the situation of Johnson? Please think about that also. Then I will not write more about him.

Hitler and Stalin

They were in a class by themselves. Supreme politicians. Doing what politicians do best. And with great exuberance. Controlling the lives and property of their victims. And making it very clear they were the ones in charge.

Hitler had more style than Stalin, who was very bland. And to a large degree stayed out of the limelight. As I remember, spending much of his time at his dacha in the country. Where his daughter Svetlana thought he was just a common, ordinary father. One who had a good job, and did not need to go to the office every day.

Serendipity strikes. I was making sure I knew how to spell "dacha" and looking for some background on Stalin. And found the most amazing article. About our subject, Stalin, and one of the great composers of the 20th century: Serge Prokofiev.

I won't repeat it here. But you might find it interesting to read. For one thing it gives some insight into what I say about who and what is important in history. Important in the sense of having created new and useful knowledge or increased individual happiness. Without a corresponding loss of that to anyone else. The essay is at:
<http://www.scena.org/columns/lebrecht/030226-NL-prokofiev.html>[27]

I found it incredibly interesting. And very sad. It is easy for those who do not live through something or under certain conditions. To say they would have "stood up for what is right" and to have not been a toady to anyone. But I know what it is like to be in a country that has just had a "coup", and the streets are filled with tanks. And you are stopped at checkpoints. To hear the machine guns killing students at a university. And to be the "guest" of the secret police for weeks.

It is a gross understatement to say "it is not a pleasant experience". Although decades have passed, I still have the occasional "flashback". To the feeling at the time that I might very well die there. Either soon, or much later, simply by virtue of being "forgotten in the system". With no one knowing where I was, and thus could do nothing about it. Even assuming they had the ability to do so.

Obviously I did get out. But there is also the knowledge years later that I just barely made it. I was later told that the day I arrived in another country they had come for me again. And only believed I had escaped their grasp the night before when showed a flight manifest with my name on it. Which they could then verify by the record of their own people at passport control.

Tens of millions of people are said to have died under Stalin. In purges, the Gulag, as a result of hunger and malnutrition. Not including the Second World War, which he

---

27 *Stalin: his final victim*, by Normal Lebrecth. February 26, 2003.

trition. Not including the Second World War, which he did not start.

Yet as I say there is one good thing about a Stalinist régime. There will be no doubt there is a dictator. And his wishes and desires for his life and yours. Those wishes and desires are the only "law" you need to know. And there is only one interpretation: his. You do not do anything against his wishes. Which may actually be quite simple. And then you can do almost anything else in life you wish. There is none of the uncertainty of democracy. No 5:4 votes on anything. It is always 1:0.

This sharpens the survival skills of the individual. Making them relatively "fit" for life. None of the mushiness of being lulled into believing you are free when you are not. As in a democracy. I am sure you realize I am being acerbic? And that I do not agree with the concept of a dictatorship? Even with the dictator operating within the cloud of fallacies of a democracy.

Stalin and Hitler are now almost universally agreed to have been bad people. Even as and for politicians. Do I need to really say how many died at their hands?

Yet please think in *principle*. And remember that when one person is killed by another—except in a true case of self-defense—it is murder. And so our modern mass murders such as Aznar, Blair, Bush, Howard, Johnson and others are no less demons and criminals that others named here.

Napoleon

Perhaps an odd person to put here. A man of great style. The uniforms! The gala balls! The right hand in the vest. The hats! And what an incredible court. Especially when there is musical accompaniment.

And the biographies! Hundreds, probably thousands of them. The encyclopedia entries. Tens of pages. While less than one for Isaac Newton. Maybe only a couple for Tesla. Whose work lights and powers the modern world. The computer on which I am writing.

And think of the legacy of Napoleon! Yes, please do think of it. Millions dead. Most in the prime of their life. Vast amounts of property destroyed. France—and Europe—impoverished for a century.

Yet Napoleon is almost idolized. Especially by those rulers who sought to emulate him. There is something wrong with a society and the supposedly thinking beings of whom it is composed. When the people believe that the life of a Napoleon is something to be glorified. Worse, emulated.

Saddam Hussein idolized and sought to emulate—even outdo—the ancient rulers of Mesopotamia. And, incredibly, Salah al-Din, better know as Saladin. Who was not a brutal tyrant. But in fact someone who respected life. Under whose rule Arabs, Christians, Jews, Muslims and others were free to worship as they wished.

And when he retook Jerusalem from the Christian knights who had butchered everyone they encountered (including other Christians), his warriors attacked only Christian knights. And after the battle he allowed all civilians—and the surviving Christian knights—to leave if they wished.

Napoleon was not only a serial killer. He also used the weapons of mass destruction of his day. A supreme politician. And magician. Having everybody believe he was "great" and important. When the opposite is true. Suppose he was not a politician. Would he have been allowed to do what he did?

Yet anyone can become a politician, yes? Simply go out into the streets. And rouse the rabble. Become a rabble-rouser. By simply promising to give the people what they want and think they need. The régime makes more mistakes than the rabble rouser. And soon he becomes the new head of the régime. A politician in his own right. And now what he does is legal because it is so written. Even the things he did in the past may now be legal.

Now those readers who are ladies should be happy that I am always using the masculine "he", yes? Rather than feeling I am sexist. But in fact I think I am sexist. I favor ladies over men. And especially because of all the tyrants of history. I have a hard time thinking of one who was female. It seems that women feel—generally speaking, and with a few modern exceptions—they have better and more important things to do in life than seeking to control the lives and property of others.

And while Margaret Thatcher was still in reality a dictator she was not unkind. And was "*relatively* right" and more competent that her predecessors or successors. Except for Winston Churchill. Who, while still a dictator, was defending his property and that of his "neighbors". Against one of the great tyrants of all times.

Churchill was not a saint. He was still a politician. And he had made some very serious mistakes in the past and did during the Second World War. But you must remember something: 1939-1942 were dark and desperate days. Mostly unfelt and unnoticed by Americans until 1942.

Hitler came very, very close to "annexing" Great Britain. And would have done so were it not for the RAF and Churchill's "bulldog image". Hitler must have had that image in mind and the words of Churchill's speech about the reception Hitler would get on the beaches if he dared make the crossing. Causing Hitler to finally turn East and to his doom.

It is for this reason and this reason alone that I list Churchill as an important man in history. The *only* politician to be to be designated as "*important* in history". All others are at best "*insignificant* in history".

There is a simple way to know if a person was important in history. Ask yourself—and others if you wish—how life would have been without that person. For politicians it is always "better".

Prime Ministers of Israel (1966-present)

All criminals of the first magnitude. First in creating and operating the vast concentration camp known as Palestine or the "occupied territories". No different in principle than a Nazi concentration camp. The "ovens" are now supplied by the American political régime and its ruler. Substituting 250 or 500 lb bombs or laser-guided missiles. The temperature is much higher, plus there is the added "value" of the explosive factor.

How many tens of thousand have died? And millions who have lost their entire life time?

When all it would have taken was for one of the prime ministers to call for a return to the 1967 borders and the restoration of land, homes and businesses to individual Palestinians. And there would have been no *9-11.* No Afghan or Iraq war. No *Bali I* & *Bali II.* No Madrid and London train bombings.

And nothing for *Dour Leader* to do except to try to make the school, healthcare and pension systems work.

Chapter 10

The Sentencing

The ultimate disaster for an individual thinking being is physiological death. The death of the body and mind. Currently, because of relatively low biological knowledge, this is an irreversible event. If we survive as a viable specie this will not always be so. And of course individual life spans will be much, much longer than now. Ranging in the millions of years. But that is another subject in another book...

Our primitive societal system based on coercion tries to use the fear of death as a weapon to prevent private crime. Crimes committed by other than political criminals. With the latter comprising the largest number of deaths. Although it is the deaths caused by private criminals that seems to occupy our minds the most. And especially the subject of the death penalty.

Which in some religions seems almost to be seen as a "wonderful" event. I once had a friend who was not a "Westerner" and not a Christian. And thus English was not the first language. I was asked the English word for someone who had died in war. I knew the word they were looking for: martyr. But perversely I said "dead". Because I do not subscribe to the idea that a person gains something or has a "benefit" by dying.

Death is the "great nothing". Which brings with it the question of why you were ever born if it is only to die. To not see light again. To hear beautiful music. To feel the touch of a loved one, and be able to touch them. To watch a beautiful sunset or breath the fresh mountain air. Scented by the pine trees. To be able to experience the joy of having created something new and useful.

To "punch the air" as a result of the feeling of exhilaration of that shot of self-esteem. Somewhat like a football player does when they have made a goal. I have even done that on occasion when a great new idea unexpectedly springs from the fingers on the keyboard.

Or in the middle of the night when, as a result of background processing activities, there is an "alert". As my semantic memory has generalized something and is preparing to ship it to the cerebral cortex. To wake up, be conscious during the event. And write down the idea before I forget it.

What does all this positive stuff and thoughts of life have to do with the sentencing of politicians for what they do? For their non-achievements and the acts that create a false feeling of self-esteem? For the blackness and death of their world.

It gives a clue to the appropriate punishment for their acts. For something that is worse than physical death. It is the awfulness of being irrelevant in life. For having no poll rating whatsoever. For the living of a worthless life. Worse than that: one of negative value.

If memory serves me correctly, which it does not sometimes these days—a "sentence" passed by low biological technology—there was an English saying about "sending a person to Coventry". A situation in which an individual was cast out of the group. No one would talk to them. It was as if they were not there. To be ostracized or shunned by the group.

This is the severest sentence that can—and should be—given to the political serial plunderers. Those who plunder the lives and other property of their victims. To in a sense make the criminal homeless. A homeless wanderer. Similar to those made physically homeless by politicians and political action. This is moral.

It is not moral to take the life of a person regardless of their crime. Even if their actions have resulted in a million dying, as with George W Bush and Saddam Hussein. Two people who accomplished the same thing by different means. Is or was Saddam worse than Bush by virtue of a difference in the style and reason for killing? Is the life of Bush "better" because he is a Westerner, a staunch Christian or a white man? As contrasted with Saddam not being a Westerner, but being a Muslim and of "mixed" color?

As I have pointed out, it is Bush who is colored. As white is the presence of all colors. Whereas black is the absence of color.

The only thing that is needed is to remove their name from the credit registry. Or perhaps leave the name, with the only data being "unknown". It is a bit like a person who has lived outside of their own country for decades. And does not even have a credit record. Their name does not even exist in the system. They have no credit because in a sense they do not even exist.

This would be the appropriate "sentence" for someone such as Bush and Saddam. When they wish to have electricity or telephone service and there is a credit search it returns "does not exist". And how could an electricity or telephone service company provide their service to a person who does not exist? And such a person would have no need for road and street services. For food and entertainment.

Yes, as today, there might be those who for some reason felt sorry for the homeless.

And when such a person no longer has access to the levers controlling the police powers of the state… or is no longer "commander in chief"… they can not be a threat to anyone. All the better when there is no system that even allows such a thing. So the temptation to be a criminal no longer exists.

Do not execute or otherwise punish them. The punishment of knowing they are a non-entity is the supreme punishment. That their name will not appear in the history books. No statues in the park, no streets, airports, buildings or motor ways named after them. I think the Richard M Nixon Parkway in Southern California has reverted to another name?

It would be a waste to have a library. Who would come to it? Who would pay for it? Who would staff it?

As I hinted above, it is a virtual court with virtual justices. No need to exact tributes from people to pay for it.

Maybe some aspiring graphics arts student could make avatars of those from the *Axis Powers*? And others who have committed crimes against humanity. The avatars on a pedestal with their name. They would remain there for viewing for a time. A "standing in state" prior to consignment to history.

But then the avatar—and with it their image—would be gone. With only the name remaining. To note the commission of a crime for which there could be no restitution. That such a person once existed, but they have disappeared into the *underworld.* From where no one returns.

Unlike the *twilight zone*, where those who go may possibly be able to atone for their crimes over time.[28] The political non-entities live in the Orphean World.[29]

In a way I have made light of this, but it is anything but funny. It relates to importance in history and to the concept of immortality. The subject of another book. And to the survival of the specie. The subject of all my books.

---

28 With credit to the writer and narrator of the wonderful fantasy TV series of the same name, Rod Sterling.

29 With credit to Henri Meilhac and Ludovic Halévy, who wrote the original text. And Jacques Offenbach for the opera and the wonderful music for *Orpheus in the Underworld.*

Appendix A

Definitions

Version 1: 2007, April

Many of these definitions were first proposed by Andrew J. Galambos. To whom I owe a tremendous amount of gratitude for their creation and for making them available to me. I have added a number of definitions created by myself. To the extent that definitions are correct this should be to the credit of Galambos. When a definition is proven to not be correct that should be for my account.

I am trying to maintain a database of definitions, but this depends on having a host for the application. Which is a system not in the public domain and requires a special server over which I have little or no control. It may be working or not working.

You can check to see if it is working and possibly look at the latest definitions. If it is working you will be redirected to that server.

<http://universal-salvage.org.uk/definitions/>

Absolute

"That which is independent of arbitrary standards of measurement".

Aristarchus

"The proper name for the planet currently referred to as Earth".

With credit to Andrew J Galambos (1924-1997), the creator of this idea. Aristarchus of Samos (310-230 bce) was one of the first to accurately determine the size of the planet.

Bias

"A preference based on discrimination".

See "Discrimination" and "Prejudice".

Bush War

"A preemptive military strike in which the aggressor loses the war and the country attacked descends into civil war. Which is hailed as a great victory by the aggressor".

George Orwell would probably call this a "double". The Ignorant One has both engaged in *doublethink* and confirmed Orwell's statement that "politics is the defense of the defensible". With *doublethink* meaning the ability to hold two contradictory concepts in the mind at the same time and accept both of them.

Capitalism

"The societal structure that protects all forms of property completely".

Coercion

"Any attempted and intentional interference with the property of another."

Communism

"A quasi-economical system under which the political state controls the lives and property of all the people and claims to own all property".[30]

See "Socialism" below.

Competence

"A measure of the number of things tried related to successful outcomes".

I have proposed the *Shackleton*[31] as the unit of competence. With 10 *Shakletons* being total, complete competence. Perhaps in the same sense as the Carnot Engine. Representing an unattainable objective?

---

30 Ownership is a moral concept and can not be achieved through coercion or fraud. By immoral means. Thus those who claim to own property but merely control it—such as the political state—do not own it. As they acquired their control through immoral means.

31 In honor of Ernest Shackleton, the great Antarctic explorer. A man of supreme competence.

Confidence

"Belief that something will happen based on rational reasons and valid thought processes".

Ant. *Faith*

Copernicus

"The proper name for our local star, which we currently refer to as 'Sun'".

As proposed by Andrew J. Galambos (1924-1997), the creator of the thought. In honor of Nicolas Copernicus (1473-1542), the creator of heliocentric hypothesis.

Crime

"A successful act of coercion".

Crime Against Humanity

"The societal condition that exists when one individual is allowed to interfere in the property of another or the act of doing so".

The problem is that once this interference in and control of the lives of others is agreed to be acceptable, there is not limit and end to it.

Critic

"A person who complains about the way something is done or the result but who can propose no better way of doing it and/or improving the result".

A critic is one of the more despicable classes of people.

See "Reviewer" below.

Democracy

"A political system wherein the ruler and ruling party faction are replaced by majority vote".

See "Political System" below.

Diplomacy

"Organized lying and conspiratorial deal making the reduces the quality life for all."

Discrimination

"The act of choosing or selecting".

Thus, any person who does not discriminate is not thinking.

See "Bias" above.

Dictator

"Anyone who controls the life and property of another thinking being".

Thus, all politicians are dictators.

Dictatorship

"A political system wherein the ruler is replaced by force".

See "Political System" below and "Democracy" above.

Equality (in a societal sense)

"Born and existing under the laws of nature, and having unrestricted access to nature".

Fair

"Any act that does not involve coercion or fraud."

Faith

"Belief that something will happen based on irrational reasons and invalid thought processes".

Freedom

"The societal condition that exists when every individual has 100% control over their own property".

Globalization

"The societal condition that exists when any individual may trade with any other individual based solely on mutually agreed terms and conditions".

Good (Absolute)

"Anything is an absolute good that is a subjective good to at least one person, but which does not involve the exercise of coercion".

Good (Subjective)

"Any phenomena, process, or action that an individual prefers".

Government

"A mechanism that provides services that protect property".

History

"A presentation of past events".

See "Positive History" below.

Hypothesis

"A suggested explanation for the cause of an event or phenomenon".

It may or may not be right on an absolute basis, and thus become a theory. Hypotheses become theories when validated through the epistemological concepts and steps of what is commonly known as "The Scientific Method". As outlined by Galambos, adding the concept of "rightness" to The Scientific Method allows it to be used in validating knowledge concerning volition.

Humanist

"Someone who believes in and lives by the ethical doctrine of humanism".

See "Humanism" following.

Humanism

"The ethical doctrine that each individual is responsible for the moral conduct of their own life".

Human Rights

"The individual's right of freedom of access to the universe, and the sanctity of property".

Illegal

"That which a political state decrees or states is not legal".

The concepts of legality and illegal are intellectual fiction. In an advanced, rational, and durable society the words would only be known to some historians. People in general would not believe the concept if you tried to explain it to them.

Impossible

"Any contemplated or attempted action that would result in the violation of a law of nature".

See "Possible" below.

Importance

"A measure of the total amount of property morally created".

Injustice

"When there is a crime for which there is no moral and rational recourse".

Intellectual (An)

"A thinking being who trends toward rational thought".

This of course eliminates most people commonly thought to be "intellectuals". And elevates many of those not thought to be an "intellectual" to that position.

Intellectual Honesty

"The ability to accept a theory which—by definition—is right on an absolute basis, when it conflicts with currently held beliefs on the subject".

Interfere

"The act of interference".

Interference

"Any action that diminishes the value of property as determined by the owner of the property".

Justice

"The condition that exists when all injustices are eliminated".

Kepler

"The proper name for the planet we currently refer to a 'Mars'."

As proposed by Andrew J. Galambos (1924-1997), who is the creator of the thought. In honor of Johannes Kepler (1571-1630).

Lawmaker

"Anyone who plans or approves unnatural [political] laws that result in interference in and control of the lives and property of their victims".

Since this is a criminal act, the individual performing it is a criminal. And is engaging in a "crime against humanity". Further, if this involves and act of war then they are involved in serial killing and perhaps genocide.

Legal

"That which a political state permits a person to do".

Level Playing Field

"The societal condition that exists when anyone can do anything they wish to do that is moral".

The concept is the cherished objective of altruists worldwide. But perhaps not this definition? Which is a proper, *right* definition. See "Right" below.

Libertarian

"A person who believes in total freedom for each and every individual".

Liberty

"The societal condition that exists when all individuals have total control over their own property".

Measure (political)

"A proposed unnatural [political] law".

See "Lawmaker" above.

Monarchy

"A political system wherein the ruler is usually replaced by a family member upon the death of the current ruler. Either natural or otherwise".

See "Political System" below.

Money (Political)

"A medium of exchange created by or the use of which is authorized and required by a political state".

Money (Rational and Moral)

"A medium of exchange used in a free market".

Moral

"Any action that does not involve intentional interference in the property of another individual".

Nation

"A political entity".

National

"Of or pertaining to a nation".

From the Latin "nation," basically meaning an ethnic group or "tribe". A tribe being what originally separated a group of people and made them different from each other.

Nationalist

"One who believes in and practices nationalism".

Nationalism

"The failed unethical doctrine that the only viable societal system is one based on coercion. With a ruler and ruling party faction to control the lives and property of all".

Natural

"Pertaining to the laws of nature"

Non-Volitional Sciences.

"The area of knowledge related to inanimate nature".

Oberth

"The proper name for our local moon".

With credit to Andrew J. Galambos (1924-1997), the creator of the thought. In honor of Hermann Oberth (1894-1989), who in the 1920s designed a liquid-fueled rocket that could take us there, and proposed a design for a "Lunar Excursion Module".

Patriot

"Anyone who adds to the quality of individual life without interfering in the property of another thinking being".

See "Traitor" below.

Play

"The act of self-enjoyment performed after the act of production".

See "Production" and "Re-Creation" below.

Policy Maker

"Someone who conspires to create unnatural laws that will produce interference in the property of another thinking being".

Political System

"A societal system based on coercion."

See "Democracy," "Dictatorship" and "Monarchy" above.

Positive History

"The version of a historical event that tells the true cause and result of the event".

Possible

"Any proposed act or action that does not violate a law of nature".

Please note that this has nothing to do with the *probability* or *plausibility* of something happening. Or of the knowledge related to how to do something.

Thus, electricity and computers were not *impossible* during the time of the Roman Empire, It is just that no one had yet discovered and elucidated the laws of nature related to the concepts.

Prejudice

"A previously held bias".

See "Bias" and "Discrimination" above.

Production

"The act of creating tangible or intangible property".

Profit

"Any moral increase in happiness".

Isn't that definition created by Andrew J. Galambos beautiful? It brings back to respectability a word that has fallen into disrepute. A nice, simple statement of "Thank you" for an action can be profit. As can a smile or a sunset.

Property (General)

"Individual man's life and all non-procreative results thereof".

This carries with it the concept that children are not property. Rather, a parent has a contractual relationship with a child. To nurture, educate and support them to the point where they can independently perform the responsibilities and obligations of individual thinking life.

Primordial Property

"Individual life itself".

The physiological body of an individual thinking being. What I like to think of as "the environmental support module for the brain." Which of course includes the brain.

Primary Property

"The thoughts of an individual that become ideas".

Beliefs, opinions, theories, the concept behind inventions or products, etc.

Secondary Property

"The tangible result of moral result of individual life".

Those tangible assets created or acquired through moral action.

Re-Creation

"The act of creating a product".

Tangible or intangible. This replaces the current word and dysfunctional concept of "recreation." Which should now be refereed to as "play." See above.

Reviewer

"A person who creates and presents a non-critical review of something".

See "Critic" above.

Right

"That which is based on true premises, valid and logical thought processes, in which the resulting action is moral".

Science

"The totality of all organized, right knowledge".

Slavery

"Seizure or control of the property of an individual without their consent".

Or,

"The societal condition that exists when someone controls the life and property of others".

Socialism

"A quasi-economical system under which the political state controls the lives and property of all the people and claims to own most of the property".

See "Communism" above.

Sovereign Entity

"And individual who has total control over their own property".

Stealing

"The seizure of the property an individual without their consent".

Terrorism

"Intentional interference in the property of another individual".

After all, might this not induce terror in the victim? And how much interference is required for an attack on property to constitute "terrorism"? One-third of a person's property? Or 100%? Or the property of more than two people? Or more than seventeen people? Thousands? Millions?

How about simplifying it as the definition states?

Theory

"The explanation for the cause of a phenomenon or event that is right on an absolute basis".

Traitor

"Anyone who follows the dictates of a political state or its ruler".

Treason

"Any act that interferes in the property of another thinking being".

True

"That which is observable".

With the senses, such as vision, hearing, smell, taste, etc. And in order to be "true" it must be observable by any other person in the same place at the same time under the same conditions.

Valid

"Having a conclusion derived from true premises".

Volition

"The characteristic of being able to reason, to make choices and value judgments, and to take action based on that process".

Volitional Science

"The study of the area of knowledge related to the societal structures of a thinking specie".

Commonly and imprecisely called "social sciences" which, as practiced on this planet at this time, is neither "social" nor "science".

Voting (moral)

"The act of selecting a product or service which you can return or dispose of when and if you wish, and which will not have an adverse effect on the lives and others".

Voting (political and immoral)

"The act of selecting a product or service which is virtually impossible to return or dispose of when and if you wish, and which will have an adverse effect on the lives of others".

War

"An organized, legal conspiracy to engage in terrorism".

It is organized, isn't it? By definition it is legal. While dictionaries use modifiers such as "secret" and "unlawful," the basic root meaning is to "breath together." To be together and to agree together to do something.

But does any of this change the principle and the morality? Once it is agreed that under certain circumstance it is OK to kill other people and destroy their property you have opened a "Pandora's box" of immorality and obfuscation. Which can only increase.

War Lord

"Anyone who works for a political régime and controls those known as 'soldiers' or 'fighters' whose mission is to destroy people and property".

Appendix B
The Quotations

Version 1: 2006, April

I believe that simply by reading these and sitting back and thinking about them a person should be able to understand much more about our societal structure. About history. And begin to see the true cause of our societal problems. Maybe even the cure.

I have many other interesting, useful, thought-provoking quotations in my database. And I am sure there are many others I do not know about and do not have.

The following are not arranged in any order…

Victor Hugo (1802-1885)

"There is nothing so powerful as an idea whose time has come."

John Locke (1632-1704)

"New ideas are always suspected, and usually opposed without any other reason but because they are not already common."

An Essay Concerning Human Understanding. (1690, dedicatory epistle)

Isaac Newton (1642-1725)

"If I have seen further than others,
it is because I have stood on the shoulders of giants."

Letter to Robert Hooke – February 5, 1676.

* * * * *

"I do not know what I may appear to the world,
but to myself I seem to have been only like a boy
playing on the sea-shore and diverting myself
in now and then finding a smoother pebble or a prettier shell than ordinary, whilst the great ocean of truth lay all undiscovered before

me."

from Brewster, *Memoirs of Newton*, [1885] vol II, ch. 27

As Galambos pointed out, Newton's must important creation was not his laws of motion or optics. But rather his statement that "... the universe is comprehensible". And directing us to the epistemological pathway to comprehend the universe. That of the Scientific Method. Which also allows us to validate existing knowledge. To determine rights in the non-volitional world.

Then Galambos created a farther account. Saying that simply by checking the morality of any action we can apply the Scientific Method to the solution of societal problems. A "simple" but very elegant and important concept.

Albert Szent-Gyürgyi von Nagryapolt (1893-1985)

"Discovery consists in seeing what everyone else has seen,
and thinking what no one else has thought."

Publication not known

Thomas Paine (1737-1809)

"A long habit of not thinking a thing wrong,
gives it a superficial appearance of being right,
and raises at first a formidable outcry in defense of custom.
But the tumult soon subsides.
Time makes more converts than reason."

Thomas Paine, Introduction to *Common Sense*, Penguin Books, 1983, p. 63

* * * * *

"O ye that love mankind! Ye that dare oppose, not only the tyranny but the tyrant, stand forth! Every spot of the old world is over-run with oppression. Freedom hath been hunted round the globe. Asia, and Africa, have long expelled her. Europe regards her like a stranger, and England hath given her warning to depart. O! receive the fugitive, and prepare in time an asylum for mankind."

Common Sense [1776], by Thomas Paine

"In England a king hath little more to do than to make war and give away places; which in plain terms, is to impoverish the nation and set it together by the ears. A pretty business indeed for a man to be allowed eight hundred thousand sterling for, and worshipped into the bargain! Of more worth is one honest man to society and in the sight of God, than all the crowned ruffians that ever lived."

Common Sense, 1776

* * * * *

"The heathens paid divine honours to their deceased kings, and the Christian world hath improved on the plan by doing the same to their living ones. How impious is the title of Sacred Majesty applied to a worm, who in the midst of his splendour is crumbling into dust."

Common Sense, 1776

* * * * *

"Men who look upon themselves born to reign, and others to obey, soon grow insolent; selected from the rest of mankind their minds are early poisoned by importance; and the world they act in differs so materially from the world at large, that they have but little opportunity of knowing its true interests, and when they succeed to the government are frequently the most ignorant and unfit of any throughout the dominions."

Common Sense, 1776

* * * * *

"It is an affront to truth to treat falsehood with complacency."

Publication not known.

* * * * *

"Taxes are not raised to carry on wars,
but wars are raised to carry on taxes."

Publication not known

* * * * *

These are the times that try men's souls. The summer soldier and the sunshine patriot will, in this crisis, shrink from the service of his country; but he that stands it now, deserves the love and thanks of man and woman. Tyranny, like hell, is not easily conquered; yet we have this consolation with us, that the harder the conflict the more glorious the triumph. What we obtain too cheap, we esteem too lightly; 'tis dearness only that gives everything its value. Heaven knows how to put a proper price on its goods; and it would be strange indeed if so celestial an article as Freedom should not be highly rated.

The Crisis, by Thomas Paine. December 23, 1776.

Jonathan Swift (1667-1745)

"When a true genius appears in the world, you may know him by this sign, that the dunces are all in a confederacy against him."

Publication not known

Hermann von Helmholtz (1821-1894)

"The originator of a new concept...finds, as a rule, that it is much more difficult to find out why other people do not understand him, than it was to discover the new truth."

Publication not known

George Bernard Shaw (1856-1950)

"The reasonable man adapts himself to the world, but the unreasonable man tries to adapt the world to him—therefore, all progress depends on the unreasonable man."

Publication not known

J. E. E. D. Acton (1834-1902)

"Power tends to corrupt and absolute power corrupts absolutely."

Letter to Bishop Mandell Creighton, 1887, April 3

* * * * *

William of Occam [Ockham] (1300-1349)

"Entia non sunt multiplicanda præter necessitatem."

[No more things should be presumed to exist than are absolutely necessary, or, Entities should not be multiplied unnecessarily]

Quodlibeta Septem, [c. 1320]

Francois Marie Arouet [Voltaire] (1694-1778)

"It is forbidden to kill; therefore all murderers are punished unless they kill in large numbers and to the sound of trumpets."
Philosophical Dictionary

"Si Dieu n'esistait pas, il faudrait l'inventer."
[If God did not exist, it would be necessary to invent him.]
Source not known

Publius Cornelius Scipio (236-183 bce)

"No man should rule other men, and certainly not for a lifetime."
Said when, as a result of his victory over Hannibal at Zama in 202 bce during the Second Punic War, he was offered the rulership for life of the Roman Empire. The empire he had created. He turned it down, accepting only for the normal one year period.

Christian Morgenstern (1871-1914)

"Das Offensichtliche ist das, was man nicht sieht, bis jeman es erklärt."
[The obvious is that which is not seen until someone first explains it clearly]
Publication not known

Richard Greenspan (dates unknown, current era)

"People who have learned something as the truth don't particularly like to hear that they've based their careers on things that were either incomplete, or not completely correct.".
Gary Taubes, "An Electrifying Possibility," *Discover*, April 1986, p. 37

Anatole France (1844-1924)

"Ignorance is the necessary condition of life itself. If we knew everything, we could not endure existence for a single hour."

Jules Henri Poincaré (1854-1912)

"Science is built up with facts, as a house is with stones.
But a collection of facts is no more a science than a heap of stones is a house."

Benjamin Disraeli (1804-1881)

"To be conscious that you are ignorant is a great step to knowledge."

Herbert Spencer (1820-1903)

"Science is organized Knowledge."

William W Morgan (Contemporary...)

"The limits of growth are found in the minds of small men."

* * * * *

"A prayer a day keeps rationality away."

* * * * *

"In true capitalism there are no guarantees of success. There is only the guarantee of the full, unhindered right to try for it, and be compensated according to the results."

* * * * *

"What a tangled web we devise,
when first we subsidize."

* * * * *

"Freedom and democracy are mutually exclusive concepts. In a political society based on the concept of democracy, true individual freedom can not exist. In a free society, the concepts of a political society based on democracy would be unthinkable. There would be no market demand for the concept."

"The Grail for which the Knights of the Roundtable searched--and for which all volitional beings search--is not just truth as they thought. But truth combined with validity and morality, which then become rightness."

This thought occurred to me while watching "Excalibur," John Boorman's interpretation of Malory's Arthurian legend.

* * * * *

"Generally speaking, the importance of a public speaker bears an inverse relationship to the number of microphones into which he or she speaks."

* * * * *

"The longer and more extensive is the interference in the free market process, the more difficult and traumatic is the return to freedom, sanity, and morality."

* * * * *

There is a direct connection between morality in a volitional society and individual physiological immortality."

* * * * *

"There is an inverse relationship between the importance of a new idea, and the ease and time in which it is understood, accepted, and implemented."

* * * * *

"The supreme act of fraud and witchcraft for politicians and the political mechanism--and especially for proponents and apologists for the concept of democracy--is in controlling the lives and property of their victims while at the same time having them believe they have freedom and are free."

"Belief in the concept of democracy as the way to freedom requires the acceptance of the idea that freedom can only be obtained through the mechanism of a minority of people controlling the lives and property of others."

This conforms to the Marx, Engels and Lenin concept, yes? When they said the political state would "wither away" and there would be the "rulership of the proletariat." Which I think is the same as "majority rule"?

* * * * *

"The chaos and disorder that will occur on a society is inversely proportional to the amount of individual freedom in that society."

* * * * *

There is a direct relationship between the attempt to eliminate uniqueness and the attempt to impose equality in volitional societies, and the level of frustration and violence that will ensue

* * * * *

In a Monarchy the chant is: The King Is Dead. Long Live the King;
In Democracy the chant is: The Incumbent is Out: Long Live the Incumbent.

Under both concepts the individual is out but the system continues. How many Kings have there been in history? How man Political Presidents? How many societal problems have we solved under the system of regulating individual behavior through coercion?

* * * * *

"As the number of sovereign entities in an area approaches the total population something interesting happens: It is called freedom."

There is only one job security: "The ability of an individual to perform a task or tasks currently in demand in the marketplace at an acceptable market price."

*****

Production compensation must be based solely on the market value of error-free production.

Henry Fielding (1707-1754)

"He in a few minutes ravished this fair creature, or at least would have ravished her, if she had not, by a timely compliance, prevented him."

> [This reminds one of the poor taxpayer and "voluntary" compliance. Except with taxes you are presented with a false alternative. You are ravished in both cases, even when you do pay "voluntarily"]

If you are interested you can access my quotations database at:

<http://universal-salvage.org.uk/quotations/>

I can not guarantee it will always work, but at the least this address should provide some information on it…

Appendix C

Bibliography

You may view this bibliography on-line as an HTML document and thus be able to simply click on the book links. Also, if there are later revisions to this bibliography they will be available there. The link:
<http://universal-salvage.org.uk/books/>

This will take you to the publisher's "Reader Index," from which you may access book revisions, bibliographies and other such things.

Rethinking the War in Afghanistan
by Gary Leupp
<http://www.dissidentvoice.org/Aug05/Leupp0824.htm>
August 24, 2005

The War in Afghanistan
Excerpted from Lakawala lecture, New Delhi
On-line version with notes, prepared Dec. 30
By Noam Chomsky
<http://www.zmag.org/lakdawalalec.htm>

The Mainspring of Human Progress
By Henry Grady Weaver
The Foundation for Economic Education,
Irvington-on-Hudson, NY (1999)
ISBN: 1-57246-064-4
<http://universal-salvage.org.uk/other_books.php#main>

Brave New World
By Aldous Huxley
Perennial Classics, HarperPerennial
First Perennial Library Edition, 1966
ISBN: 0-06-09287-1
<http://universal-salvage.org.uk/huxley_orwell_books.php#brave>

Nineteen Eighty-Four
By George Orwell
A Signet Classic, Penguin Books Ltd, England
ISBN: 0-451-52493-4
<http://universal-salvage.org.uk/huxley_orwell_books.php#1984>

The Discoverers
By Daniel J. Boorstin
Vintage Books, Random House, NY
ISBN: 0-394-72626-1
<http://universal-salvage.org.uk/other_books.php#boorstin>

Natural Right and History
By Leo Straus
University of Chicago Press
ISBN: 0226776948
<http://universal-salvage.org.uk/general.php#leo>

Evolutionary Origins of Morality
Edited by Leonard D. Katz
Imprint Academic (March 1, 2000)
ISBN: 090784507X
<http://universal-salvage.org.uk/general.php#morality>

The Discovery of Freedom
By Rose Wilder Lane
50th Anniversary Edition
Fox & Wilkes, San Francisco, California (1993)
ISBN: 0-930073-21-5
<http://universal-salvage.org.uk/other_books.php#free>

Economics in One Lesson
By Henry Hazlitt
Three Rivers Press, NY
ISBN: 0-517-54823-2
<http://universal-salvage.org.uk/other_books.php#econ>

A Greater Than Napoleon
By B. H. Liddell Hart
Da Capo Press, New York
ISBN: 0-306-80583-9
<http://universal-salvage.org.uk/scipio_by_about.php#hart>

Cowardly New World
By William W Morgan
Universal Salvage Corporation, Escondido, California
ISBN: 1-4196-2610-8
<http://universal-salvage.org.uk/book_list.php>

Colours of Infinity: The Beauty and Power of Fractals
by Nigel Lesmoir-Gordon
Clear Books
ISBN: 1904555055
<http://universal-salvage.org.uk/general.php#colours>

The Journey of Man: A Genetic Odyssey
By Spencer Wells
Random House
ISBN: 0812971469
<http://universal-salvage.org.uk/general.php#journey>

The Image: A Guide to Pseudo-Events in America
By Daniel J Boorstin
Vintage Press
ISBN: 0679741801

The Seekers
Daniel J. Boorstin
Vintage Books, A division of Random House (1999)
ISBN 0-375-70475-2
<http://universal-salvage.org.uk/general.php#seekers>

A Short History of Almost Everything
By Bill Bryson
Broadway Books, NY (2003)
ISBN: 0767923227
<http://universal-salvage.org.uk/general.php#bryson>

The Internal Constitution of the Stars
By Arthur Stanley Eddington
Cambridge University Press
ISBN: 0521337089
<http://universal-salvage.org.uk/eddington_by_about.php#internal>

Stellar Structure
By Arthur Stanley Eddington
<http://universal-salvage.org.uk/eddington_by_about.php#stellar>

Sir Isaac Newton: His Life and Work (Paperback)
by Edward N. Andrade
Publisher: Doubleday (January, 2000)
ISBN: 038502326X
<http://universal-salvage.org.uk/newton_by_about.php#sir>

The Life of Sir Isaac Newton
By David Brewster
<http://universal-salvage.org.uk/newton_by_about.php#life>

A God Against the Gods
by Allen Drury
ISBN: 0385001991
<http://universal-salvage.org.uk/other_books.php#allen>

An "Einstein" Thought Experiment: Rationality & Morality Waves in Nature
By William W Morgan
ISBN: 0-9778492-0-1
<http://universal-salvage.org.uk/book_list.php>

Sic Itur Ad Astra
By Andrew J Galambos
ISBN: 0880780045
<http://universal-salvage.org.uk/galambos_pubs.phph#six>

Index

H

I

J

K

M

N

O

P

R

S

T

U

V

Z

Made in the USA
Monee, IL
04 November 2026

67386986R00066